THE DRAMATIC LIFE OF
A POWERFUL AND ENIGMATIC LEADER

THE EMPRESS

THE DRAMATIC LIFE OF
A POWERFUL AND
ENIGMATIC LEADER

THE EMPRESS

Kalyani Shankar

BLOOMSBURY
NEW DELHI • LONDON • OXFORD • NEW YORK • SYDNEY

ISBN 978 93 86606 04 4
2 4 6 8 10 9 7 5 3 1

Bloomsbury Publishing India Pvt. Ltd
Second Floor, LSC Building No.4
DDA Complex, Pocket C – 6 & 7, Vasant Kunj
New Delhi 110070
www.bloomsbury.com

Typeset by Manipal Digital Systems
Printed and bound in India by Thomson Press India Ltd.
To find out more about our authors and books visit www.bloomsbury.com.
Here you will find extracts, author interviews, details of forthcoming
events and the option to sign up for our newsletters.

The book is dedicated to my granddaughter Annika.

PREFACE

This is an updated version of the Jayalalithaa chapter from my earlier book 'Gods of Power'. I have been following Tamil Nadu politics for more than three decades as a journalist and have personally witnessed some of the events described in the book.

This is a political profile of the late Jayalalithaa Jayaram, the Chief Minister of Tamil Nadu, who was a cult figure. It was not easy to understand her cult status and her persona, as she was an enigma. She was a political personality to reckon with; not only at the regional level but also on the national stage. She returned to power four times despite allegations of corruption and was the accused in several court cases. She was even convicted by the Supreme Court in the Disproportionate Assets case after her death.

The book portrays her legal struggles, her politics, intrigues, and the ups and downs in her political as well as personal life. It analyses how she tackled these challenges and came out strong. The book will be of use to researchers especially as it is based on interviews with primary sources.

I wish to thank all those who had given me access to information and insight about Jayalalithaa including Tirunavukkarasu, Dr Subramanian Swamy and Bhishma Narain Singh. My special thanks to former Chief Editor of the Hindu N Ravi for giving permission to use some of the rare photographs. Last but not least, my thanks to Bloomsbury, India, for publishing this book and the help given by the CEO Rajiv Beri and his team.

CONTENTS

Preface   vii

Prologue   xi

A Cult Figure?   1

Early Years   4

Beginning of A Political Career   8

Relationships   11

Entry into Politics   13

Jaya's Political Life after MGR   29

Jaya: The Woman with An Iron Will   64

Towards The End...   100

Postscript   106

Larger than Life   108

Shoes too Big to Fill   114

Sasikala Takes Over   116

Endnotes   130

PROLOGUE

I was watching Jayalalithaa Jayaram on television, in a rare interview. It was an eloquent performance. My niece, sitting beside me, was also keenly watching the show. At the end of it, she declared, 'I would vote for her.' She has no knowledge of Tamil Nadu politics, or about Jaya, for that matter. She lives in the United States but has become an instant convert. Such was Jaya's charisma!

One was reminded of a statement made by a senior police officer from the Karnataka cadre: 'Whoever meets her, be it an Indian or a foreigner, cannot but come back impressed. She is like that—imperious in her own way, but impressive. To be imperious is not easy for all.' Jaya, apart from being charismatic, induced fear in people. Many of those who were approached in connection with this book, including the All India Anna Dravida Munnetra Khazagam (AIADMK) Members of Parliament (MPs), were afraid to talk about her on record. While some bluntly refused, others agreed to speak only off the record of the enigma called Jayalalithaa. From filmdom to politics, her life remains an interesting subject of study and observation.

The AIADMK was a party floated by film star- turned politician M.G. Ramachandran on 17 October 1972, as a breakaway party from the Dravida Munnetra Kazhagam (DMK), a Dravidian party. The AIADMK, under MGR's leadership, came to power soon, and he became the Chief Minister of Tamil Nadu. He retained this position for ten years—from 1977 to 1987, until his death—winning three consecutive Assembly polls held in 1977, 1980 and 1984.

It was MGR who initiated Jayalalithaa into politics and also promoted her, since 1982. After MGR's death, in 1987, the party split into two factions—one headed by Jayalalithaa, and the other by MGR's wife, Janaki. But after the 1989 Assembly polls, in which Janaki got just two seats while Jaya secured twenty-seven, Janaki gave up and the party was united under Jayalalithaa.

Coalitions headed by the party have won the polls to the Tamil Nadu Assembly seventeen times so far, and it has alternated in power, with the DMK, for the past three decades. Jayalalithaa was heading the party when she died on 5 December 2016. Under her leadership, the AIADMK came to power four times: 1991, 2001, 2011 and 2016.

A CULT FIGURE?

Jaya more than fulfilled the requirement of a cult figure; she was a crowd-puller and 'vote-catcher', largely on the basis of her charismatic appeal. Her fans held prayers in temples during her phases of ill health and legal troubles. During her last days, they fasted, and even tonsured their heads. There were attempts to self immolation and death as they camped outside her house and hospital in a show of devotion and loyalty to their goddess. Politically, she attracted devoted supporters, and was able to convert the crowds into votes for her party. This characteristic of hers was visible even during her lowest phase, when she was facing several legal charges. There would be huge crowds waiting to get a glimpse of their leader when she appeared in court; and they were dejected when she was put behind bars twice.

Washington Post, paying tributes to her after her death, quoted her as saying: 'At any given point of time, I did what had to be done,' she said in a television interview. 'I never stopped to think whether I'm a man or a woman ... I felt I had to do this, I did it, I did whatever I felt was right.'[1]

A Wikileaks telegram sent from the US embassy in Chennai to Washington, in 2009, described her as behaving like empress of the South, on her way to conquer the rest of India: 'A man brought her into politics but she rose to the height of power on her own, breaking new ground for women as she went along. Known as Tamil Nadu's "Iron Lady", she is famous for her toughness. Her autocratic style has led to a complete domination of her political party, whose followers fawn over her with slavish displays of obedience to her commands. She has succeeded in Tamil Nadu's male dominated political environment by literally reversing traditional stereotypes. Jayalalithaa is widely seen as the toughest, most muscular political figure in the state. She has leveraged this image of strength into political power, serving multiple terms as Chief Minister to a state of more than 65 million people and demonstrating that India's women can make a mark on their nation's politics.'[2]

Another telegram from Chennai to Washington notes: 'Jayalalithaa is the consummate autocrat. Her total domination of the AIADMK is legendary. A prominent Congress party official described the Tamil Nadu political parties this way: "The DMK isn't a party, it's a social movement. Congress isn't a party; it's a mob that comes together for elections. And the AIADMK isn't a political party, it's a personality cult." Jayalalithaa casts a huge and menacing shadow over her party. Even in private meetings with Consulate officers, AIADMK leaders never call her by her name; they call her "Amma"(Tamil for mother), "Madam", or "our Leader." Their offices, vehicles, and homes are festooned with multiple pictures of Jayalalithaa. Senior AIADMK leaders, especially men, used to physically prostrate themselves before her to demonstrate their obeisance. Jayalalithaa has since started to discourage the practice after the English language media began to mock it.'[3] If this is not personality cult, what else could it be?

However, the BJP leader Dr Subramanian Swamy, who was heading the Janata Party earlier, and had an 'on now' and 'off now' relationship with Jayalalithaa, argues, 'I don't think she practices a personality cult. Her party survives on two scores. A very large section in Tamil Nadu, which is opposed to Karunanidhi or the DMK, supports her. The people associate her with MGR. Women are her main strength. She has nothing else. Otherwise she would not have lost the Assembly elections in 1996. So many leaders with corrupt personalities have also won, while a tea-shop owner defeated her.' Swamy adds, 'Despite her intelligence, she is totally under her friend and companion Sasikala's thumb. According to me, she is not an independent person.'[4]

Jayalalithaa herself felt that she was a much misunderstood person. 'I have been portrayed as a tough and formidable character. Some would call me a Veerangana (a warrior woman). To tell the truth, I am a very soft and kind-hearted person but life has placed me in very difficult situations. I have been surrounded by a whole set of adversaries, all coming at me with various kinds of weapons. I could not lie back and allow myself to be annihilated. The feeling I got then was: Why should I allow myself to be eliminated just because certain people don't like me?'[5]

For many, she was insecure, mercurial and suspicious. According to Jaya, it was her circumstances that made her who and what she was.

EARLY YEARS

ailing from the celluloid world, Jaya's life story runs like a screenplay. She excelled in two fields: films and politics. She was introduced to films by her mother and to politics by her mentor and AIADMK supremo, M.G. Ramachandran, himself a superstar.

Born to Vedavalli and Jayaram on 24 February 1948, Jayalalithaa hailed from a Tamil Iyengar family, originally from Srirangam, in Tamil Nadu, but they later shifted to Karnataka. Jayalalithaa's given name was Komalavalli, and this was changed to Jayalalithaa when she was one year old; her pet name was Ammu. Jaya spent her childhood in Mysore and Bengaluru (erstwhile Bangalore). She lost her father, Jayaram, a lawyer by profession, when she was barely two years old. It was her mother, Vedavalli, who brought up both the children: Jayalalithaa, and her brother, Jayakumar.

Jaya's mother, also known as Sandhya Jayaram, was a film actress and the child used to accompany her at times to the studios, during school holidays. By sheer chance, she became a child actress. In her own words: 'When I was just seven years old, I was in Bangalore during the summer vacation. My mother was acting in a Kannada film, *Srisaila Mahatmyam* (Glory of Srisaila); I had gone to the studios with her. The child artiste who was to play Goddess Parvathi fell ill. The producer and director saw me with my mother and asked her whether she would allow me to play that role. My mother agreed. That was the first time I used make up and appeared before the camera.'[6]

Jaya's childhood was unusual; there wasn't much opportunity to play and run about like other children. A strict regimen had to be followed. 'I was carefree only till the age of four. From then on, I had to rise at five in the morning and there would be a teacher to teach me classical vocal Carnatic music. After that I would leave for school, which used to last until 4 p.m. in the afternoon. I was given instructions not to stay back and play with other children. I was to come straight home and even before I could enter the front door, there would be two dance teachers waiting for me. Of course, I would glare at them but they would be unmoved,' continued Jaya on the one-to-one show on television.[7]

Jaya passed her matriculation examination with flying colours from the prestigious Sacred Heart School, Church Park, Chennai. After winning a gold medal for securing a top position in academics, she would have liked to continue her higher education for which she also won a scholarship. She never wanted to be a film actress or a politician. Her dream was to become a lawyer. She wistfully noted: 'If I had been allowed to study and have my way, I would have been up there in the legal firmament along with Nani Palkhiwala, Ram Jethmalani, Fali. S. Nariman, Kapil Sibal and several other legal luminaries.'[8] However, this was not to be! Chubby as a child, Jaya blossomed into a stunning teenager, and plunged into acting in films.

Jaya recalled that when her mother persuaded her to join films. 'For three days, there was a royal battle at home. I wept, I raged, I argued. But what can one do when one is sixteen? I was just a child and I couldn't run away from home. And then mother explained the family circumstances to me. She told me that she was not getting too many film offers. My grandfather had retired. We had to support my grandparents, my aunt and her children, and my brother hadn't completed his education. So my mother made me understand that there was no other way out really, and that I had to earn and support the family. So when she explained the family circumstances to me, I was, to put it mildly, shocked. Because until then I had the impression that we were very wealthy. My mother had never allowed her worries to bother me or my brother. Right from the time we were born, we grew up thinking we were millionaire's children. My mother gave us the best of everything. Anything we wanted was there the next day. So we never really knew or understood how much she had to struggle to give us this kind of an upbringing. So when I finally understood, my whole attitude changed. Then I felt a lot of sympathy for my mother. And I thought mother had been through enough struggle and mother had suffered so much in her life that I felt it wasn't fair to expect her to keep on struggling for our sakes. Then I thought it was my duty to provide relief to my mother, and take on the burden of supporting the family. So that is when I told mother to return the scholarship, and accepted the film offers that had come our way. But everything was handed to me on a golden platter. Offers were pouring in by themselves. So she said make use of it, why not take it.'[9]

She made her debut in a Kannada film, *Chinnada Gombe*, directed by the famous producer B.R. Panthulu, in 1964. The following year brought her glory when she acted as a young widow in C.V. Sridhar's *Vennira Aadi* (White Clothes). She played the role of a schizophrenic widow, and the stunning newcomer became an instant rage. When Jayalalithaa was first cast opposite MGR, in a film called

Ayirathil Oruvan (One in A Thousand), he was forty-eight years old and she was only seventeen. Despite the age difference between the two protagonists, the film became a super hit. The lead pair went on to appear together in twenty-eight more films out of which twenty-four were box office bonanzas. In 1973, she won three Filmfare awards for *Pattikada Pattanama*, (Village or City) *Suryakanthi* (Sunflower), and *Sri Krishna Satyam* (The Truth about Lord Krishna). For Jaya, there was no looking back and she soon took to acting in Telugu films as well.

Jaya acted in more than 150 films in Tamil, Telugu, Malayalam, Kannada, Hindi and even an English movie, *The Epistle*. More than seventy-five of these ran for more than a 100 days each in theatres and eight were silver jubilee (twenty-five weeks) hits. She won seven Filmfare awards and six Tamil Nadu Cinema Fan awards for best actress. She became the highest paid actress in the Tamil film industry in 1966 after eleven consecutive hits that year. Jayalalithaa herself claimed that she was good in doing whatever she did. 'I didn't like it. But when I decide to do something, whether I like it or not, I give it my all. I must excel in it. I must do it superlatively well. So, though I hated my career in films, though I was the number one star of my time, and though I really shouldn't say I don't like politics, people say I'm a successful politician, and a good one. I'm surprised at myself.'[10] Besides a career in films, as an actress as well as a film producer, Jaya was also a columnist, a short story writer, and a novelist.

BEGINNING OF A POLITICAL CAREER

The sudden death of her mother, Sandhya, in 1971, shattered Jaya. She felt a void, and for some time thereafter, she distanced herself from the cine world and even shifted base to Hyderabad. Dr Swamy recalls, 'She left MGR and went off with Shoban Babu, a Telugu superstar. Things were patched up once again and she returned to MGR later.' After this break in relationship with MGR, until 1980, she returned to the limelight, once again, but this time into politics.

MGR was the matinee idol who joined the Dravida Munnetra Kazhagam; he was also one of their prized political showpieces. He used his films to send social messages across to the people. He often played Robin Hood in his films, helping the poor by robbing the rich. He was one of the most popular Tamil leaders who held sway over the state of Tamil Nadu from the Sixties onwards to the day he died, in December 1987. MGR is still worshipped by his fans. He brought Jayalalithaa into politics in 1982, when he felt he needed someone trustworthy to go round on his behalf and meet people. On her part, Jayalalithaa sought votes in his name until as late as the recent 2016 Assembly polls.

With a shift in ground, from adversary to admirer, Dr Swamy gives a glimpse of Jayalalithaa's persona from both sides of the fence: 'She is extraordinarily intelligent and has a very quick grasp of things. If she had continued her studies, she would have been a scholar. But she had been brutalized in the cinema world. They took advantage of her poverty. Then her mother was also forcing her to act.'[11]

Confirming this, the late R.K. Kumar, Jaya's chartered accountant, who was close to her at one time, and was her political party's minister in the Vajpayee government, observed, 'She was probably treated badly by some people in her youth. That is perhaps why she wants to retaliate at others now, particularly the men.' Kumar had also recalled how paranoid she was in 1998, that Vajpayee might file court cases against her even before he took over as the country's Prime Minister." And that was one reason why she delayed giving the letter of support to the President. Eventually she saw reason and called me up at three in the morning and asked me to hand over the letter.'[12]

However, Dr Swamy explains that the letter was delayed because the Bharatiya Janata Party (BJP) was not making him (Dr Swamy), who was heading the Janata Party then, a minister. 'She called me at three in the morning and said, "We're not going to give the letter of support." Pramod Mahajan (BJP minister) had talked to me directly and I passed the word to her that these people were asking me for the letter. She told me that they do not want her people anywhere and she was very upset. I also advised her, "Don't pull down the government now. You should not have gone with the BJP in the first place and made speeches about a stable government. Just because of the issue of my not becoming Finance Minister you can't go back now. So make a deal with them." It was my idea.'

A former Central Bureau of Investigation (CBI) director thinks she was one of the most intelligent people he had come across. 'She is very sharp. When she listens to you she is fully attentive, her mind does not wander. You must accept that the film glamour is there too. She was a successful actress. She was a known name and a known face. These were her advantages. People who are successful in the film world have a tremendous advantage. The most important factor was her proximity to MGR. He gave important positions to her and he did project her. There was no doubt about it.'[13]

RELATIONSHIPS

Jayalalithaa had a roller-coaster relationship with MGR. She claimed to film star Simi Garewal, who interviewed her for her television show *Rendezvous*, 'He was a very warm and caring kind of a person. And after my mother died, he replaced her in my life. He was everything to me. He was mother, father, friend, philosopher, guide - everything. He sort of took over my life.'[14]

In the initial years when MGR and Jaya were on good terms, and were almost inseparable, he had renovated a luxury suite for her in Tamil Nadu Bhavan in New Delhi. The instructions to the then Resident Commissioner, Ramdass were that while she was staying at the suite, he had to take care of her every whim and fancy (he particularly narrated an incident when she threw tantrums for not getting coconut water). But when their relationship soured, and she was no longer receiving favours from MGR, and was not even allowed to talk to him leave alone meet him while he was unwell and away in New York, every time Jayalalithaa wanted to stay at the suite, he had to get clearance from MGR for the same, the Commissioner told the author.

Tirunavukkarasu, a former AIADMK minister in the MGR government, a one-time strong supporter of hers, says that, 'She was always under the aegis of somebody: First her mother, then MGR and now her companion Sasikala.

That was her inner feeling. She was not able to move around freely. All this must have created some frustration. She felt insecure.'[15]

The disenchantment with practically everyone she was close to is reflected in her autobiography published in the Tamil weekly *Kumudam*, in 1978. 'Her father is presented as a "squanderer" and a "gentleman of leisure", a man "who could not handle anything properly". MGR was a person who she said she would rather "treat as an equal rather than a superstar". A "betrayal" by a school friend too left a deep impression. Jayalalithaa had played postman for this friend who was in love with a neighbour. But "when the girl's mother discovered what was going on, my friend played Brutus and painted me as a daughter of an actress and a girl of loose morals."'[16] The magazine abruptly stopped the serial, and has disappeared from circulation altogether.

Jayalalithaa remained a spinster, despite liking the idea of marriage as any other young girl would. Why did she not marry? Did she not find anyone suitable? She had once pointed out that 'Every young girl dreams of meeting the perfect man, her Prince Charming, or marrying him and living happily ever after. I too had these dreams as a teenager, as a young girl. If my mother had got me married at the age of 18, even an arranged marriage, I'd have settled down happily in a life of domesticity. I'd have been content looking after my house, raising children. But life taught me such things don't happen to everyone. And it's unrealistic to expect happiness in life.'[17] Instead of looking after a family, she looked after a state. Often accused of throwing tantrums, Jaya told Simi Garewal: 'I'm human like everyone else. I do experience emotions and I wouldn't be normal if I didn't experience feelings of anger and other emotions but when you are a leader, you learn to control your emotions. You learn not to show them openly, you have to.'[18]

ENTRY INTO POLITICS

Jayalalithaa joined the AIADMK on 5 June 1982, and MGR was instrumental in introducing her to politics. Jaya said: 'After my mother's death in 1971, I began to distance myself from the film industry and at one stage I stopped acting in films. That gave me considerable free time to reflect on the state of affairs in the country. I felt that there was much that could be done to rectify things that were going wrong. Around 1979, MGR invited me to join the AIADMK. I was not too keen on this at the beginning. I took nearly one and a half years to make my decision. Finally in 1982, MGR appealed to me by saying he needed someone on whom he could depend upon 100 per cent.'[19]

MGR found his party losing ground in the 1980 Lok Sabha elections when the Congress–Dravida Munnetra Kazhagam (DMK) alliance swept the polls. His party (AIADMK) secured only two seats. With Indira Gandhi coming back to power, and the DMK posing a challenge to his political party and career in the state of Tamil Nadu, MGR became nervous.

The DMK is a Dravidian party founded by C.N. Annadurai, in 1949, as a breakaway faction of the Dravida Kazhagam (known as the Justice Party until 1944), headed by Periyar Ramaswamy Naicker. Annadurai became the first DMK Chief Minister in 1967, defeating the Congress.

Since his death, in 1969, M. Karunanidhi has been the chief of the DMK, becoming the Chief Minister six times.

While the AIADMK supported Indira Gandhi during the Emergency, Karunanidhi opposed it and the DMK leaders were even jailed under false implications. Indira Gandhi lost the 1977 Lok Sabha polls; in the Assembly elections held a few months later, the AIADMK came to power. MGR then decided to support the Janata Party-led Central Government and dumped Indira Gandhi. The DMK aligned with the Congress in the 1980 Lok Sabha polls while MGR went with the Janata Party and got just two seats. Indira Gandhi, who came back to power in 1980, got the MGR government dismissed. However, MGR won the Assembly elections a few months later, and came back to power winning 179 seats.

After the Lok Sabha defeat, MGR realised that he was losing touch with the people on the ground. He knew that he needed to get someone who could go around the state on his behalf and connect with the people. He was looking for a person who gave him the confidence of being able to help him out in political endeavours, and he chose his film star colleague, Jayalalithaa, zeroing in on her charisma, intelligence, and glamour. He was confident in the knowledge that Jaya was articulate, was a crowd-puller, and, most importantly, was trustworthy. He also knew that he could depend on her to share his political burden.

Though Jaya was no longer acting in films, she retained the advantage of having been a glamorous actress. People in Tamil Nadu adored their matinee idols—both Jaya and MGR—and the fact that Jaya had played MGR's leading lady in several films gave her the cutting edge, even when MGR suffered a stroke on 5 October 1984, following which Prime Minister Indira Gandhi sent him to New York for treatment.

Jaya soon acquired enormous clout, especially because she had MGR's attention. She made her first speech on *'Pennin Perumai'* (Strength of A Woman). She was appointed as a member of the high level committee overseeing the Chief Minister's Nutritious Noon Meal scheme. She found her new job fascinating, as it was a significant change from the glitter-and-glamour of filmdom into the rough-and-tumble of politics. As Mohandas, a police officer perceived to be close to MGR, wrote in his book, *'MGR: The Man and the Myth'* that Jaya was one of the few leaders in the country who possessed great fighting qualities. She first became the propaganda secretary of AIADMK, which was a very powerful position within the party.

MGR was very keen on the midday meal scheme, which ensured that school-going children got their free lunch in school. Jaya personally started supervising the World Bank -funded scheme and got kudos for its implementation. The tours undertaken by her in her role as the propaganda secretary in Thanjavur, Pudukottai, Ramanathapuram, Tirunelveli, Salem and Dharmapuri districts of Tamil Nadu, in November 1983, witnessed unprecedented crowds and a tumultuous reception, especially from the womenfolk and the rural populace. They seemed to have no reservation in accepting her as MGR's true representative. Her well-prepared speeches, her diction and clarity of thought, supported by facts and figures, highlighting the beneficial schemes launched by the AIADMK government were well received.

Despite her initial success in the political arena, Jayalalithaa struggled to fit into the Tamil Nadu politics, which was a male-dominated conservative state, and it did not show respect to film stars, especially women. With the rise of the Dravidian parties like the DMK, it also became anti–Brahmin. Jaya being a woman, a Brahmin and a film star, was therefore particularly disadvantaged. She had to keep her democratic and accommodative self in check, lest the others took advantage. After MGR's death, she became particularly vulnerable and had to fend for herself.

What worked to her advantage was the perception that she was MGR's favourite heroine. Also, the fact that she had the highest number of fan clubs among the heroines helped her find a place in Tamil Nadu politics. Interestingly, Dravidian politics centred around films. Dravidian political parties used films to send their message across to the masses. The DMK came to prominence using films as a medium to influence voters' minds. MGR became popular because he built for himself the image of Robin Hood using the medium of films to send social messages to the public. Films could always sway the Tamil Nadu public. DMK leaders C.N. Annadurai and M. Karunanidhi were powerful scriptwriters who used films to spread the Dravidian ideology. Kannadasan and Pudukottai Kalyanasundaram, both DMK members, wrote powerful lyrics. Although Jayalalithaa was not indoctrinated in the Dravidian politics, her strength was her mass appeal.

Many other matinee idols also launched their own outfits. Captain Vijaykant, a well-known Tamil film star, floated his party Desiya Murpokku Dravida Kazhagam (DMDK) on 14 September 2005. He was able to secure a ten per cent vote share in the 2006 Assembly polls. In the 2009 Lok Sabha polls, the DMDK contested all seats but did not win a single one. In the 2011 Assembly polls, by becoming an alliance partner with the AIADMK, it won twenty-nine seats and emerged as the second largest party, next to the AIADMK. However, since then, it has drawn a blank in the 2014 and 2016 polls.

Sarath Kumar, another hero, launched his Samuthva Makkal Party (SMP), breaking away from the DMK on 31 August 2007. It won two seats in the 2011 Assembly polls.

Going back to the narrative, Jaya, being ambitious, began to throw her weight around which annoyed many senior party leaders. Her detractors complained to MGR about her arrogance in a bid to check her growth. She had to fight every inch of her way up, as the senior leaders, including R.M. Veerappan, who was MGR's right hand man, were quite upset at her meteoric rise. As Mohandas observes, 'There were certain factions in the ruling party and the MGR fans' associations, which did not like her impressive inroads into politics. Their point was that she had no credentials and was too junior to be a political leader and that her right place was on the stage or silver screen.'[20]

According to him, Veerappan took him aside one night at the Apollo Hospital when MGR was hospitalised and told him that, unfortunately, it was he, who was responsible for the reconciliation between MGR and Jayalalithaa in 1981, by giving her a chance to present a dance-drama before the delegates at the World Tamil Conference held in Madurai. The two were estranged before and he (Veerappan) rued the day he brought them together, because he said, it seemed apparent that Jayalalithaa was not content to be a mere lady companion and that she fancied herself, with her convent education and charisma, to be a cut above the rest and to be the only eligible successor to MGR in the party as well as the government. R.M. Veerappan added that she was too ambitious for a new entrant to the party, and that senior and tested leaders had their reservations and misgivings about Jayalalithaa's activities ever since she was made the propaganda secretary. 'They were very happy when, at the general council meeting (in 1984) before he fell ill, MGR divested Jayalalithaa of her position as propaganda secretary. Veerappan further said this one act of MGR was sufficient to show her that he no longer trusted her and that she should, therefore, be kept out of any interim arrangement of leadership until MGR recouped.'[21]

This internal fight continued throughout MGR's later days. Senior leader S.D. Somasundaram, who had exited the DMK with MGR, and was himself a competent organiser, raised a banner of revolt against MGR. SDS, as he was affectionately called, reached a point of no return after his removal from the cabinet and formed his own party, Namadhu Kazhagam. MGR was emotionally upset about his departure as S.D. Somasundaram had a fairly clean record and MGR was fond of him. As Mohandas observes: 'The advent of a newcomer like Jayalalithaa as the powerful propaganda secretary and almost number two in the party hurt SDS (as it did other ministers and elder party leaders), who, by his seniority, simple living and general behaviour, had endeared himself to the ordinary party worker. Jayalalithaa had charisma no doubt, next only to MGR, but SDS felt she was raised to a very high position in the party because of her proximity to MGR. Others took it silently, but SDS was of a different mettle and took advantage of the slight demoralization in the party after the upsets in four by-elections, to time his quittal.'[22]

To resolve the internal bickering, MGR made Jayalalithaa a member of the Rajya Sabha in 1983, where she later became the leader of the AIADMK group. As former editor of *The Hindu*, N. Ravi, notes, 'This proved to be a launch pad for her. But initially she was MGR's shadow. She would not have thought at that stage that she would take over the party. After 1986, she proved to be very popular and the party obviously had no strong leadership. She was probably the best known and popular figure after MGR. This as well as her exposure to Delhi proved to be to her advantage.'[23] Former minister Mani

Shankar Aiyar agrees that after she went to Delhi as the Rajya Sabha member, she discovered she had far greater potential as a politician. 'She realized that she was not just a high class film actress but also a high class politician.'[24]

By this time the Congress–DMK relationship had soured and the AIADMK had come closer to Indira Gandhi. Jaya being the face of the party, Mrs Gandhi took a fancy to her and even invited her for dinner to her house. As a member of the Upper House, she started attending Parliament regularly and spoke on subjects close to her heart. Congress leader Margaret Alva, who was then the Minister for Parliamentary Affairs in the Congress government, befriended her. She continued to be in touch with Jaya, and recalls, 'I used to urge her to come to the House because whenever she attended, the attendance in the House also improved.' This was true in a sense because other MPs tried to befriend her. When the Rajya Sabha paid tributes to her after her death, deputy chairman of Rajya Sabha, P.J. Kurien noted that even Prime Minister Indira Gandhi used to come to the House to listen to her speeches, added: 'The gallery was full and when she finished speaking, everyone was praising her articulation, content and language. It made news that day.'[25] Jaya's speeches in the Rajya Sabha were noted for their incisiveness and deep understanding of the subject under discussion. She never ventured to speak on any topic unless she was conversant with and sure of all the facts. She spoke on subjects including power projects of Tamil Nadu, fair share for states in a federal polity, Centre-state relations, situation in Sri Lanka, iniquities of dowry system, plight of handloom weavers across the country, constitutional status of Jammu and Kashmir, and so on. This was the hallmark of her speeches, serving as a sort of political apprenticeship, enabling her to emerge as the Chief Minister of Tamil Nadu later.

On 5 October 1984, MGR suddenly took ill. He had a stroke and even lost his speech. He was moved to New York in a special plane provided by Indira Gandhi. She had deputed the then Foreign Minister P.V. Narasimha Rao and her special envoy G. Parthasarathy to see him off. The question now was how to run the Tamil Nadu government while the Chief Minister was in New York. Era Nedunchezhian, second-in-command in the MGR cabinet, assumed responsibility for the government's day-to-day functioning. For the running of the party, a committee was set up to oversee its functioning. The proposed committee would have necessarily included Jayalalithaa. But a large majority of the leaders was against her, for various reasons. They also pointed out that MGR himself had removed Jaya from the post of propaganda secretary and that he had expressed his disapproval of her functioning, at the general council of the party, which met just before MGR fell ill.

This was a period of darkness in Jaya's life when MGR was being treated in New York. She was even denied a meeting with him, as MGR's wife, Janaki, and senior leaders like R.M. Veerappan controlled the access. When she was humiliated, Jaya fought back. Her own brand of loyalists remained with her, including ministers like Tirunavukkarasu. Meanwhile, on 31 October 1984, Prime Minister Indira Gandhi was assassinated and her son, Rajiv Gandhi, became her successor. On 24 December 1984, Lok Sabha elections were held. The AIADMK-Congress alliance continued and even took advantage of the sympathy factor. During the election process, there was a bitter fight between the followers of R.M. Veerappan and Jayalalithaa. MGR himself was recuperating in New York, while a messenger brought in his nomination papers to Chennai. His video message from the hospital bed and Indira Gandhi's assassination were helpful for the alliance to win a majority.

At this point, the internal conflict within the AIADMK had reached a peak. Veerappan, who was calling the shots in both the government and the party, was opposed to Jaya campaigning for the party. 'But eventually wiser counsel seemed to prevail and the party die-hards accepted Jayalalithaa's offer to undertake the election tour. She diplomatically visited R.M. Veerappan at his residence and sought his good wishes for the success of her venture. Veerappan was predictably embarrassed but responded suitably. She attracted huge crowds wherever she went and it was the V sign, which also signified two leaves—the symbol of the AIADMK and the hand all the way.'[26]

Rajiv Gandhi returned with 415 seats and at the state level, the AIADMK won 130 seats of the 235 members' Assembly; the Congress won sixty-two, while the DMK got only twenty-two seats. MGR was elected leader of the AIADMK party once again and this was conveyed to the then Governor S.L. Khurana. AIADMK leaders Nedunchezhian and K. Chokkalinagam went to New York to consult with MGR over a letter received from the Governor S.L. Khurana stating MGR should nominate someone until he returned to Chennai. However, they came back soon with the information that MGR was scheduled to return in February (1985), and until then the interim government would continue.

On 20 January 1985, Jayalalithaa was removed from the parliamentary party leadership and was replaced by Aladi Aruna, who later joined the DMK. Jaya protested against this and alleged that these things were being done without MGR's knowledge. In an interview to *The Hindu*, she spoke about her removal from the leadership of the parliamentary party at a time when MGR was hospitalised in New York. She asked, 'If Mr M. G. Ramachandran was perfectly all right and was in full possession of mental faculties, and was able to understand questions and answer them and gave instructions and orders, why then are these leaders afraid to let me see him.'[27] In the days that followed, she continued to allege that MGR was not aware of what was being said or done in his name and that a small group of people were manipulating his condition for their own benefit.

Mohandas witnessed that 'Jayalalithaa did not take her being side-lined lying down. She went to town crying herself hoarse about the injustice done to her, when her election tours had a significant impact resulting in the AIADMK being returned to power. She did not spare anyone. Her ire was also directed against Janaki Ramachandran, R.M. Veerappan and other leaders who did not take kindly to her.'[28]

MGR returned to Chennai on 4 February 1985. He met the Governor on February 6, and was sworn in as Chief Minister at a secret ceremony on February 10. No other cabinet ministers were sworn in that day. True to his character, MGR kept Jaya outside his inner circle. She was denied access and given a feeling that she was discarded.

Jaya continued her struggle, as her detractors complained to MGR about her arrogance during his absence. According to Tirunavukkarasu, MGR called him and asked him for an update on Jaya during his absence. 'After seeing off the Governor, we were all standing there. He gestured to me and I went inside. He asked me what happened in his absence. By the time I started, all the other ministers who were outside thought I might talk in favour of Jaya; they sent the American doctors and nurses in. They came and told me I should not disturb him. MGR told them that it was he who had asked me in. Then Janaki also came inside and he told her also to wait outside. I started feeling embarrassed. I asked him to rest and left. He again called me later and I went with all the press clippings. Very patiently he went through the papers. He knew I was supporting her,' reveals Tirunavukkarasu.[29]

Tirunavukkarasu claims that as far as he knew, MGR never hinted or thought that Jayalalithaa could become his political heir. She was even dismissed as party's propaganda secretary and kept away from active politics during his last days. Moreover, 'After returning from the US he gave oral instructions to ministers, including myself not to go to Jayalalithaa's house or talk to her personally or over the phone. All the office bearers of the party were also similarly instructed. He was also aware of the letter she had written to Rajiv Gandhi asking him to make her the deputy Chief Minister in the absence of MGR. She had developed a rapport with the Prime Minister, Home Minister Buta Singh and others. Before his death MGR was very angry with her.'[30]

Journalist Ajit Pillai writes: '"She approached the then Prime Minister, Rajiv Gandhi, and Governor S.L. Khurana to appoint her as chief minister since she felt that MGR's health would not permit him to discharge his duties. Her moves were widely reported. Jaya's hardcore supporter and Salem MP, P. Kannan, who acted as her courier by delivering her letter to MGR explaining what transpired during his absence, while he was in New York, and brought a rapprochement between Jayalalithaa and MGR, confirmed her efforts to get to the top slot. So did Valampuri John, (another of her hardcore supporters who helped Jaya in her formative political years), Tirunavukkarsu and R.M. Veerappan. Stung by her moves, MGR stripped her of the deputy leadership of the parliamentary party. In an interview to *Savvy* magazine, she articulated her anger against the decision: 'MGR has been a great influence in my life, I don't deny that. But now I am my own person. I have evolved. Hereafter, I am responsible only for myself. Never again will anybody influence me to such an extent that all my thoughts and actions and statements are influenced and made in a particular way just because someone else wants it that way.'"[31]

Tirunavukkarasu recalls how MGR kept her out after his return from the US until his death. He did not meet her at all for about three months, nor was she allowed to meet him. Finally, the first meeting took place in the secretariat. 'She wanted an appointment and he said, "Come to the secretariat." Evidently he was not happy with her. He was suspicious of her and probably felt she was overambitious, and wanted to be the Chief Minister and party general secretary. She was insisting on being made the secretary of the MGR fans' association and wanted him to announce it at the party conference in Madurai in 1986. When he did not oblige, she was quite peeved and left for Madras the same night. He did not offer her any position—either in the party or at the MGR Manram (Fans' Association). The next morning, when I went to meet the CM, he showed me the newspapers and the publicity she got at the conference. He was quite cut up that she had left for Madras. Before his death, he was very angry with her.'[32]

MGR's sudden death on 24 December 1987 shocked the state, leaving behind a political vacuum. Although he had been ailing and his speech was affected, no one thought that the end would be so quick. Mohandas recalls a scene he witnessed when he went to see MGR's body at his Ramavaram garden early in the morning. 'When I came out of the room, I saw Jayalalithaa shouting and storming her way up the stairs—taking more than one step at a time. She was fury personified. I made a quiet exit because I had no role to play, being no longer the Intelligence Chief. Later I came to understand that Jayalalithaa was not allowed to see MGR's body, as it was taken out by the back door to Rajaji Hall where it lay in state for mourners to have a last look,'[33] Mohandas observes. Jaya ran behind the ambulance, which took the body and followed it in her car. She stood by the side of

MGR's body for thirteen hours the first day and eight hours the second day like a statue.

There were thousands of mourners and there were also some self-immolation deaths by his ardent fans. Tamil Nadu plunged into shock and grief. Many came to pay their last respects to their departed leader. Narrating the events on that day, Jayalalithaa recalled: 'I wanted to place a wreath on his body when it was placed on the gun carriage. The soldiers were kind enough to assist me to do that. I also wanted to join the funeral procession and board the gun carriage which the soldiers were helping me to do. As I was climbing the carriage, I heard shouts behind and saw MLA Dr. K.P. Ramalingam advancing menacingly towards me. Immediately, a young man in a blue shirt, who I was subsequently told was Tamil film actor Deepan, Janaki's younger brother's son, jumped on to the gun-carriage, hit me on the forehead and pushed me out. The armed forces personnel tried to help me back on top of the carriage, and again Deepan pushed me, beat me, and threw me out. I was injured and bruised all over my body. I was disgusted with this uncouth behaviour and the unparliamentary language used by Deepan and Ramalingam. I decided, much against my conscience, not to attend the funeral and came away.'[34] This author, who had accompanied a three-member ministerial delegation from Delhi deputed by Prime Minister Rajiv Gandhi for the funeral, was witness to how some members of the anti-Jaya group pushed her away. She wanted to send a public signal that she was MGR's political heir, which her detractors saw through immediately. The ugly scene, which was telecast live, really marred the solemn occasion. Jaya was trying to tell the world that she was MGR's chosen successor and claimed his political legacy from that moment. When she went home, she sent out telegrams to the Governor, Chief Secretary and other officials about the way she was manhandled. The media also played it up as front-page news and prime time television news. This public assault on her created sympathy for Jayalalithaa, and it came to her help later during the elections.

This was the turning point, which she was looking for and she snatched the opportunity. 'Yes, my growth and development started in 1984 when MGR fell ill. My adversaries in the party started to marginalise me. That was when I really had to fend for myself and it was totally so after his death,' Jayalalithaa admitted.[35] Former BJP president Jana Krishnamurthy looks at the issue in more realistic terms: 'MGR built up a personality cult. The strength of Jayalalithaa is still MGR. If for any reason she deviates from the path of MGR, people will not like it. Still his name is respected and he is adored.'[36]

Since MGR did not name any successor, there was a bitter succession fight within the ruling AIADMK. He probably felt that there was no one who was a match to his leadership. Perhaps emulating him, Jayalalithaa also did not name a successor, with the result there was a fight for her legacy after her death. DMK chief Karunanidhi recalls that on 28 December 1987, Nedunchezhian, MGR's number two in the Cabinet, announced in the secretariat that he was a candidate for the post of Chief Minister but the Governor rejected his claim saying there was no precedence. However, Veerappan staged a coup by making Janaki, MGR's successor. For her, it was more personal than political. MLAs owing allegiance to Jaya opposed this move tooth-and-nail. On the other side, Jayalalithaa, backed by the rank and file of the party, was elected as the general secretary of the AIADMK by the general body in a meeting held on 1 January 1988. She had the support of thirty-three MLAs. The result was that Janaki Ramachandran, who had the support of ninety-seven MLAs, short of a simple majority, was elected as the leader of the legislative wing of the AIADMK. Janaki paraded her faction, and Governor S.L. Khurana was satisfied, and he accepted Janaki's claim. She was sworn in on 6 January 1988. Jaya wrote to the Governor pointing out the impropriety. The Governor replied that he had given three weeks' time to Janaki for proving a majority. January 25 was the date for the Governor's address to the Assembly and January 28 for proving a majority for Janaki. Meanwhile, Jaya went to Delhi and called on Rajiv Gandhi, seeking his support as the Congress had sixty-two MLAs. Jaya's plan was at least to prevent the continuance of the Janaki government with the support of the Congress. Rajiv Gandhi, facing a dilemma, declared that the Congress would give support to the undivided AIADMK, but the party split. The Congress party decided to abstain from voting and the Janaki government fell on the floor of the House.

Former President R. Venkataraman writes in his autobiographical book, *My Presidential Years*: 'On the evening of January 24, Jayalalithaa called on me. She mentioned that Rajaram had crossed over to Janaki's side and that people thought and said that I had asked him to do so. I told her the news was totally baseless. I repeated what I had always been saying—that the rival groups should try and settle their differences among themselves. I told her also that from my position and office I could not interfere in local politics.'[37]

Karunanidhi vividly describes the ugly scenes in the Assembly in his autobiography, *Nenjukku Needi (Justice for My Heart)*. He recalls that 'On January 28, there was a big battle in the Assembly. Chappals, and soda bottles were thrown. Speaker P.H. Pandian and other members were attacked. At the last minute Congress decided not to vote for Janaki—leaving the Janaki and Jaya groups to fight it out in the House, even fist fights and breaking the mikes.

Congress, that gave support to MGR as long as he was alive, completely changed its tune after Jaya's Delhi visit. When Janaki was deserted at the last minute, she suddenly remembered the DMK. Her faction leaders, Madhavan, Rajaram and others came to my residence and requested me to support Janaki. She also spoke to me on the phone and requested me. However, I told them that we had already taken a decision not to support either group. The Indian Union Muslim League leader A.K.A Abdul Samad also requested me. I expressed my inability to change the executive decision. The Speaker dismissed 33 MLAs and announced Janaki as having won the confidence vote. The Centre dismissed the Janaki government on January 30, 1998, and imposed President's Rule.'[38]

G. K. Moopanar, chief of Tamil Manila Congress (TMC), and a Congressman at that time, recalling this incident, observed: 'Rajiv Gandhi, who was in Mizoram on that crucial night before the voting, himself took the decision not to support Janaki and had asked Pondicherry Chief Minister Farooq Marakkayar to proceed to Chennai to convey the decision to the Congress MLAs and get it implemented. People did not vote for Janaki. They said that she herself could not get elected and realized that she could not carry on as the CM either.'[39] On January 30, Governor S.L. Khurana sent a report on the incidents that took place on January 28 in the Legislative Assembly. This was sent to the government along with a recommendation on January 30 that the Tamil Nadu Assembly may be dissolved and the state may be placed under the President's Rule.

JAYA'S POLITICAL LIFE AFTER MGR

MGR's death was the turning point and a defining moment in Jaya's life and also her political career. When film star Simi Garewal asked her whether her fiercest battle was the one she fought after MGR's death, Jaya said, 'You are absolutely right because as long as he was there, he was the leader. I only had to follow his instructions. After his death I was left to fend for myself. I was left totally alone. And he didn't smoothen the way for me to become his successor. He didn't. Not like Indira Gandhi did for Rajiv Gandhi. She groomed him, paved the way so that he could smoothly move to take over as her successor. Now if you look at all the other women leaders who have made it to the top in Asia, they were all the daughters, wives or widows of former prime ministers or presidents because if you're a wife automatically so much respect is given to you. People talk about you, defer to you, with respect. But such wasn't the case with me. Though Dr. MGR introduced me to politics, he certainly didn't smoothen the way for me, he didn't make anything easy for me. I had to fight and struggle my way up every inch of the way.'[40]

She claimed that there was so much mud slung at her and she had to face so many brickbats, vilification and slander. When it came to the tribe of politicians, it was downright demeaning, insulting and humiliating. 'If you are born sensitive, you stay sensitive till the end of your life. If you are hypersensitive like I am, you feel the pain magnified a thousandfold that perhaps another person would. And then having to face this kind of slander, the kind of terrible distorted image that has been built up of me in the media. That really hurt. That's not me, that's not what I am.'[41]

The 1989 Assembly elections saw both the Janaki and Jayalalithaa factions fighting separately, and the Janaki faction suffered a humiliating defeat. Although the DMK swept the polls, 1989 was still remembered as the date for settling the succession battle of the AIADMK. While the two heroines of MGR—his wife Janaki (also a film star, before her marriage to MGR) and Jayalalithaa—claimed his legacy in a bitter battle, MGR's fan clubs were confused about whom to support. Janaki managed to get the support of another Tamil superstar Sivaji Ganesan, who left the Congress to start his own party. Jaya grasped early the nuances of Tamil Nadu politics and sought the anti-Karunanidhi votes. Janaki lost the election not only because of her lack of aggression but also due to her outright praise of MGR's arch rival Karunanidhi that an average AIADMK worker was not able to understand. By making Karunanidhi her adversary, Jaya managed to win twenty-seven seats against Janaki's two seats. Ten days after the Assembly polls, Janaki announced that she had decided to quit politics and not be a hindrance to anyone and literally handed over her faction to Jayalalithaa. The united AIADMK became Jayalalithaa's property.

Jaya became the first woman Leader of the Opposition in the Assembly, with her twenty-seven MLAs. Soon, she faced the worst humiliation in the Assembly. When Chief Minister Karunanidhi got up to present the annual budget on 25 March 1989, Jayalalithaa as the Leader of Opposition, insisted that her adjournment motion should be taken up first. This led to a melee with the DMK members shouting at her. Describing the ugly scene, Jaya recalled, 'Nothing was really worth the humiliation I suffered in the Assembly, on the floor of the Legislative Assembly on March 25, 1989 in the presence of the Chief Minister Mr Karunanidhi, with both his wives watching from the VIP boxes. All his ministers and MLAs assaulted me. They grabbed everything they could lay their hands upon, chairs, mike, a heavy brass bell on the Speaker's table. If they had succeeded in banging it on my head, I wouldn't be alive today. My MLAs saved me that day. And one of them even tried to pull at my saree. They pulled at my hair. In fact they tore out some of my hair. They threw chappals at me. They threw heavy bundles of papers, books at me. That day I left the Assembly in tears. But I was also angry. I made a vow that day. I said I would never set foot in this Assembly again as long as this man continues to be the Chief Minister. And when I enter again, I will enter as chief minister. And I fulfilled my vow within two years. I did it; I don't think this has happened to any other woman in politics. That was a bad experience.'[42] Days after the incident Prime Minister Rajiv Gandhi visited Jayalalithaa in hospital as she was was recovering from her injuries. It was the beginning of the crucial Congress-Jayalalithaa led AIADMK alliance.

The year 1989 also marked Jayalalithaa's entry into national politics. The Congress-AIADMK combine won thirty-eight of the thirty-nine Lok Sabha seats in Tamil Nadu, with the Congress winning twenty-seven seats and the AIADMK eleven seats. Jaya controlled this group in Parliament. She shared an excellent rapport with Rajiv Gandhi, and also trusted him. Rajiv Gandhi had realised that the 1989 slogan of 'Kamaraj Raj' and the decision not to go for any alliance had both not clicked with the voters. Therefore, by 1991, the Congress and the AIADMK came closer and fought the elections together, adopting the old MGR formula of sixty per cent for the AIADMK and 40 per cent for the Congress for the Assembly polls and vice versa for the Lok Sabha polls. The short-lived government of V.P. Singh, which succeeded Rajiv Gandhi, could not check the growth of the AIADMK. When the Congress Party supported the claims of Chandra Shekhar, who broke the V.P. Singh government in 1990 to become the Prime Minister, Jayalalithaa's political clout also increased because she was an ally of the Congress. She put pressure on Prime Minister Chandra Shekhar to get the Karunanidhi government dismissed. Chandra Shekhar, citing deteriorating law and order and alleged closeness of the Chief Minister with the LTTE, got the Karunanidhi government dismissed on 30 January 1991.

The assassination of Rajiv Gandhi on 21 May 1991, at Sriperumbudur, while he was on his electioneering tour in Tamil Nadu, led to the AIADMK-Congress victory in the subsequent elections. Both parties did well in the Lok Sabha and Assembly polls, which were held simultaneously. Jaya secured 169 out of the 234 seats in the Assembly and became the Chief Minister of the state. She was sworn in as youngest ever and the second woman Chief Minister of Tamil Nadu on 24 June 1991. As mentioned earlier, the first woman Chief Minister was MGR's wife V.N. Janaki, who ruled for twenty-four days in January 1988. Her government fell when she could not prove her majority, resulting in the state falling under the President's Rule.

Since then, both Karunanidhi and Jayalalithaa succeeded each other as CMs for most of the last three decades and also played vendetta politics against each other. Tirunavukkarasu notes: 'I think Jayalalithaa does not have any personal vote bank. That is my feeling. Although the party split and there were other smaller parties, she was the only one fighting the DMK on the anti-DMK platform. It has always been the DMK or the AIADMK. The supporters of the DMK cannot vote for the AIADMK and vice versa. She was the only leader for the AIADMK and they had no choice or alternative. But it is still MGR's vote bank. Even now MGR's name sells and women are still with MGR. People do not know that MGR was not for Jaya as his successor. The wrong perception was that he brought her into politics to succeed him. MGR's pro-AIADMK votes are 20 to 25 per cent and these are still intact. These are anti-DMK and anti-Karunanidhi votes. Despite all the corruption charges and cases, Jaya still has 25 per cent of core voters intact. The two-leaf symbol is also important, since it is associated with MGR.'[43]

Former Congress leader G.K. Moopanar also agreed that MGR's two-leaves symbol still counts in Tamil Nadu. He notes that 'MGR had his own constituency, which cannot be replaced and MGR assiduously nurtured this constituency.'[44] K. Subramanian, who became the advocate general of Jaya's government when she took over as the Chief Minister, recalls: 'The two groups had filed petitions claiming the two-leaves symbol. Janaki fought the elections with the two-pigeon symbol, while Jaya had the cock symbol. After the elections when the Janaki faction was wiped out, Jaya's people called up Muthuswamy of the Janaki faction and the unification move of the two groups became successful. Janaki filed an affidavit for withdrawal. I appeared before the then Election Commissioner, Peri Sastry. It was a Saturday evening when he released the 'two leaves' symbol. He told me, "This is the first time since Independence that I am releasing a symbol that was frozen." He pronounced the order. Monday was the last day for filing nominations for the two by-elections—Mannargudi and Marungapur. Jaya fought with the two-leaves symbol and won both the seats. This was just a month after the Assembly elections in which DMK had swept the polls. That gave her the MGR magic wand.'[45]

A government official recalls how MGR left a deep-rooted impression on the people. 'Once I saw a bundle of silk lungis lying in his room when I had gone to see him. Bangalore was famous for silk lungis. He told his security man he would take all of them. He went inside and came out with a bundle of notes. I asked him, "You came only yesterday. Why is so much money required?" His security officer said, "No sir, when he is here, he insists on paying for everyone who is with him including his security, pilot car driver—that they all should eat at his cost." This was his habit even at his Ramavaram garden residence. That showed his concern for the people . . . I was talking about the lungis. He returned within a month again. This time also he bought quite a big bundle of lungis. I asked him the reason. He told me that he had taken only one. The rest were distributed to the people in his garden, working for him. That was his large heart. MGR told me, "I know what hunger is. I spent many hungry days." Having known hunger, he knew what poverty means. That is how he thought of the mid-day meal scheme. Years after he died, I was once travelling in Tamil Nadu. I used to stop near a teashop and ask the people about the mid-day meal scheme. They would say MGR was giving them meals. People thought he had real concern for them.' Since people thought that Jayalalithaa was MGR's political heir, their votes were transferred to her.

Jayalalithaa came to power on a triple sympathy factor. She inherited the two-leaves symbol that poor Tamils hold dear, connecting it with MGR. In 1989, she was humiliated in the legislature when DMK ministers allegedly tried pulling at her saree, leading to a huge scandal. In 1991, her alliance partner Rajiv Gandhi was killed by the Liberation Tigers of

Tamil Eelam (LTTE), just before the elections. LTTE chief Velupillai Prabhakaran feared that if Rajiv Gandhi came back to power, as it was speculated, the LTTE would be wiped out. These three factors boosted her political career in an unprecedented manner.

The role of the Tamil Nadu political parties in raising the issue of the Sri Lankan Tamils must be mentioned here. Tamil Nadu is separated from Sri Lanka by a narrow 20-kilometer strip of sea, known as the Palk Straits. Tamil Nadu had always shown concern about its Tamil brethren across the Palk Straits, while political parties have used it as a political tool, especially during elections. This attitude of the Dravidian parties made leaders like Jayalalithaa, Karunanidhi, and others take positions towards the Centre; while they were partners in Central coalitions, they also put pressure on the Union government to influence its Sri Lanka policy.

Tamil militant groups in Sri Lanka were demanding a separate Tamil Eelam. Under Prime Minister Indira Gandhi's leadership, these groups were provided with not just training on Indian soil, but also arms. They would often cross the sea and come into Tamil Nadu, which was hospitable to them. When the separatist groups found it difficult to remain in Sri Lanka, they made their base in Tamil Nadu. According to one estimate in the 80s, about 20,000 Sri Lankan Tamils, including about 1,000 suspected rebels, found a safe haven in the state.

Indira Gandhi and MGR worked in tandem on the Sri Lankan Tamil issue. Initially, MGR supported the LTTE rebels and even funded them. Indira Gandhi sought the cooperation of MGR to deal with the LTTE chief, Prabhakaran, as did Rajiv Gandhi, even before the Indo-Sri Lankan accord of 1987. It was a peace accord signed in Colombo on 29 July 1987 between Indian Prime Minister

Rajiv Gandhi and Sri Lankan President J.R. Jayewardene. The accord was meant to resolve the Sri Lankan Tamil ethnic issue by enabling the thirteenth amendment to the Constitution of Sri Lanka and the Provincial Councils Act of 1987. Under this agreement, Colombo agreed to the devolution of power to its provinces, the Sri Lankan troops were to be withdrawn to their barracks in the north, and the Tamil rebels were to surrender their arms.

Rajiv Gandhi, prior to the signing of the accord, persuaded MGR to come to Delhi and influence the leaders of the Sri Lankan militant group Liberation Tigers of Tamil Eeelam (LTTE), which was fighting a guerilla war against the Sri Lankan government. Rajiv Gandhi also met the LTTE leaders who were brought to Delhi before he reached Colombo for signing the accord. When Prabhakaran went back on the accord, acceding to the Sri Lankan government's request, Rajiv Gandhi sent the Indian Peace Keeping Force (IPKF) to deal with the LTTE and other rebels.

The IPKF was formed on the mandate of the Indo-Sri Lanka accord and it remained in Sri Lanka from 1987 to 1989 to disarm the militant groups. It was inducted on the request of President J.R. Jayewardene. Soon, to enforce peace, the IPKF began to get embroiled in clashes with the LTTE. Both sides fought fiercely, resulting in heavy casualties on both sides. The IPKF began to withdraw at the request of President Premadasa who succeeded Jayewardene in 1989. Meanwhile, V.P. Singh succeeded Rajiv Gandhi in 1989, in India. MGR distanced himself after the accord, and after his death in 1987, the LTTE turned to Karunanidhi who became a partner in the V.P. Singh coalition government in Delhi. Karunanidhi was soft on the LTTE and put pressure on V.P. Singh to withdraw the IPKF, which was fighting the LTTE on behalf of the Sri Lankan government. Meanwhile, the people of Tamil Nadu got disenchanted with the activities of the LTTE. The militants ran amuck, and the people turned against them. The assassination of Rajiv Gandhi on 21 May 1991, for which the LTTE was found responsible, resulted in more anger amongst the people of Tamil Nadu.

The first thing Jaya did after the assassination of Rajiv Gandhi was to order a crackdown on the LTTE. A Wikileaks telegram notes that 'a bureaucrat who held a key security portfolio at that time said Jayalalithaa ordered him to do "whatever it takes to finish off the LTTE in Tamil Nadu, even if it required extra judicial killings of LTTE associates in the state."'[46] She showed the same iron will while ordering the killing of sandalwood bandit, Veerappan. The dacoit was on the most wanted list for sandalwood and ivory smuggling. He was operating freely in the forests of Tamil Nadu, Karnataka and Kerala. As *India Today* notes: 'In the pantheon of Indian dacoits, not even Malkhan Singh or Phoolan Devi earned the nationwide notoriety that Veerappan had. He had also gained a certain degree of political clout by buying influence with his money.'[47]

Jayalalithaa served as Chief Minister—from 1991 to 1996, 2001 to 2006, 2011 and 2016 until the time of her death—with two short breaks in her second and third terms. She became the first incumbent Chief Minister who had to step down following conviction in a Disproportionate Assets (DA) case on 27 September 2014. She was sentenced to four years of jail in 2014, and a fine of Rs 100 crores by the trial court. However, the Karnataka High Court acquitted her and she triumphantly came back to office on 23 May 2015. Jaya won a landslide victory in the 2016 Assembly polls, coming back for a second consecutive time, a feat which had not been achieved by any political leader for decades in Tamil Nadu.

Jayalalithaa came to power at a crucial time in the history of Tamil Nadu. Law and order was in a deteriorating condition, with the LTTE militants roaming around freely in the state. People wanted change, and a stable government. Although Jaya was new to administration, she began her term as Chief Minister rather well. Governor Bhishma Narain Singh recalls how she was keen to be a good administrator. 'Throughout my period as Governor of Tamil Nadu, she used to come to me every week or ten days and discuss with me all the problems of the state. I administered oath to her on June 21, 1991. When she came to see me the next day, it was not a long meeting. I gave her a list—law and order, LTTE and the economic situation. She was glad that my list was short. She was Chief Minister for the first time. Her meetings with me were very fruitful. I never told the press what we discussed. When she met me, it was she who used to talk. She began telling everyone that the Governor was a true friend, philosopher and guide. She had a good impression of me. How to prevent militancy, how to speed up development— these were the issues Jayalalithaaji and I discussed. She was quick to learn. On one occasion, I pointed out to her that one of her ministers had a corrupt image. She took immediate action and dropped him promptly. Again when on the university amendment, the file was sent to me at the last moment, I wanted some amendments. The bill was to be introduced the next morning and I had no time to discuss with her. There were others who told her that I was going beyond my limit but she sided with me and said what I had done was right.'[48]

Commenting on her intelligence and a comprehensive grasp of issues, Singh adds: 'If you explained to her she understood very quickly. I had suggested to her that she should have good relations with the Centre. After that,

I don't know what went wrong, since I lost touch after relinquishing governorship. I met her only at her foster son's wedding . . . She is perceived to be a different person now.'[49]

Power went to her head after she sat in the Chief Minister's chair at Fort St George. Jaya's imperious attitude came to the fore even during her dealings with successive Prime Ministers. Once she flew into a rage when Vincent George, Rajiv Gandhi's private secretary, did not put her call through to the Prime Minister. She was calling him from Chennai, in 1989 and since Rajiv had already retired for the day, George did not connect her with him. At that point of time, she was the Leader of the Opposition in the Tamil Nadu Assembly and her annoyance made headlines.

Late Digvijay Singh, Chandra Shekhar's Minister of state for External Affairs recalled an incident. Jayalalithaa, who was then an MLA, visited Chandra Shekhar when he was the Prime Minister. Jaya sat in the waiting room at 7, Race Course Road, the Prime Minister's residence, and Chandra Shekhar was busy in an emergency meeting with the then Finance Minister Yashwant Sinha, in January 1991. Jaya got impatient and rose to leave. Digvijay Singh then went inside and informed the Prime Minister, who sent word to her to wait for a few minutes. But she left in a huff.

Her abrasive behaviour with Narasimha Rao when he was the Prime Minister (1991-1996) was equally well known. She came to Delhi in 1993, camped for three days before she severed her party's alliance with the Congress, called the editors of newspapers and made allegations that Rao was asking her to favour his people in contracts and other deals. There was mistrust between the two of them. And former Prime Minister Atal Behari Vajpayee, too, had to put up with her tantrums before she pulled down his government in 1999. She was so rude that on one occasion, in May 1999, when Vajpayee was in Chennai at the invitation of the Marumalarchi Dravida Munnetra Kazhagam (MDMK) chief Vaiko, the BJP's coalition partner, Jaya left the city to avoid meeting him and came back early next morning before the PM left. She did not care to see him off despite being a partner in his government. The author was a witness to this embarrassment, being a part of the media group accompanying the Prime Minister. Her anger was compounded when the then Chief Minister Karunanidhi had lined up his entire cabinet to receive the Prime Minister.

Talking about her experiences with various Prime Ministers, Jaya once said: 'With prime ministers I have generally felt exasperated because of the delay and vacillation. I am known for being bold and decisive and I always want quick action. Now there is a multiparty government at the Centre (referring to the Manmohan Singh government), one has to train oneself to deal with it. There are 12 ministers from Tamil Nadu at the Centre whose single point agenda is to constantly denigrate my government. Prime Minister Manmohan Singh is an excellent person and a great economist. I respect him a lot but I feel his hands are tied when it comes to reining in his ministers especially those from Tamil Nadu.'[50]

Jaya remained a mystique: Inaccessible, and creating an aura around herself. She never courted the media or wrote letters to her followers. She communicated in the simplest possible way, each word carefully chosen, and delivered with precision. However, she had well imbibed and imitated the MGR style—in politics as well as in personal life. After all, she had been a glamorous and successful film star, albeit an elusive one. Like MGR, she, too, remained an enigma. Where she went wrong was her disconnect with the people. While MGR used to meet the party workers in his house as well as at the AIADMK party office frequently, Jayalalithaa made herself inaccessible.

She would keep people waiting for hours, and eventually not see them at times. Her behaviour, even with party members, reflected a typical cult culture. There are eyewitness accounts of an Assembly Speaker, P.H. Pandian, who, after being sworn in, prostrated before her in the Tamil Nadu Assembly, in public. Few in her party called her by name; she was respectfully referred to as amma, madam or *thalaivi* (leader). MGR was called *puratchi thalaivar* (revolutionary leader); she was called *puratchi thalaivi* (woman revolutionary leader), its feminine equivalent. Like MGR, she, too, was referred to as *Idhaya Deivam* (God or goddess of the heart). Jayalalithaa discounted all these reports that she encouraged her party members to pay obeisance to her in public: 'I have asked them several times not to do it. But you must understand that touching the feet of elders is part of the Indian culture. If they insist on doing so, what can I do? There have also been ministers who never fell at my feet, never prostrated themselves and yet I gave them due respect and honour.'[51]

It was mandatory for all her MPs, MLAs and party workers to carry her photograph in their pockets in a manner in which could be seen. Although they went through the motions of elections, it was Jaya who appointed, removed, transferred, promoted, demoted, expelled and recruited members and workers at her own discretion. Ministers were appointed, fired or shuffled according to her whims. She alone decided who qualified as AIADMK candidates, because they were elected in her name. Therefore, it didn't matter who she chose every election. She denied reports that there was only one chair on the dais in her public meetings—for her. On whether she terrorized party workers as part of her tactics, she had a ready defence: 'I am a very strict person. I am very organized and very efficient. I expect the same efficiency from people who are working with me to perform well. I don't think that is a crime. I was like a mother to them,'[52] she stated in that television interview.

She never allowed anyone to come close to her or take advantage of his or her proximity to her. In short, through her failures and successes, she learnt that the power lay in the hands of the masses. She was also very well aware of the impermanence of power and the fickle nature of political alliances. Even when surrounded by a mass of people, she knew she was all alone at the top. Jaya wondered how all kinds of stories were spread and intense speculation vis-à-vis her life was so rife! She blamed it on a male-dominated society: 'The only explanation is that ours is still a male-dominated society. Perhaps people cannot bear to see the reign of a woman. Perhaps people cannot bear to see a woman emerge as a powerful leader. That could be the only explanation. I cannot think of anything else,' she said, and added: 'By and large, I have been given a bad press. Those who really got to know me always felt I am a very likeable and friendly person . . . I was not inaccessible as the Chief Minister. I took my work seriously and really did my work conscientiously, which left me very little time for the media and to meet people. This was probably construed as being inaccessible.'[53]

Dr Swamy seeking out the duality in her personality notes, 'She was brutalized and has a Dr Jekyll and Mr Hyde sort of personality. Once she wants something, she is most amiable. Once she thinks a person's utility is over, she will dump him.' Tirunavukkarasu too agrees entirely with Dr Swamy and recalls how she gradually became arrogant. 'She always had a dual character. One side of her is very pleasant. The other side is arrogant, ferocious and short-tempered. Even MGR knew of this side, Rajiv Gandhi knew, Narasimha Rao knew and Vajpayee also knew. She created problems pressurizing them. I am reminded of what Madhavan, the person who was with the family during her childhood, used to say. When she was in school, all the other children used to come to their cars. But she would simply stand and someone had to go and fetch her. Even while shooting for her films, she used to take the car and go and someone had to go and fetch her back. After coming to power, she became even more arrogant.'[54]

Jayalalithaa was impulsive. A senior police officer recalls her visit to Kumbakonam, 273 kms from Chennai, in south Tamil Nadu. It is a temple town with many important temples located in and around it. As the Chief Minister, on 18 February 1992, she took an impulsive decision to visit the place along with her associate, Sasikala, to take a holy dip in the auspicious Maha maham tank. Twelve Shiva temples are connected with the Maha maham festival which is held in Kumbakonam once in twelve years. The Chief Minister was keen on attending the Maha maham festival because her birthday fell on that day (under the Maham star in the Tamil month of Masi, a day that is considered auspicious to take a dip in that particular temple tank). A stampede took place because the space meant for pilgrims had become restricted, since it had to be used for Jayalalithaa's security. She later admitted to this police officer that her officials did not guide her properly.

Another incident, proof of her impulsive behaviour, took place in 1993, when she registered her protest on the Cauvery river water dispute issue in a dramatic way. One of her close associates, a legal luminary, recalls how one fine morning, without telling anyone, she took a chair and rushed off to the Marina beach in Chennai without her security. The Chief Minister squatted near the MGR Samadhi.

The Chief Secretary got a phone call about her sitting in protest and then the pell-mell started. The whole city was agog with the Chief Minister herself taking recourse to such a step. Her demand was that the Centre should appoint a monitoring committee to oversee implementation of the Cauvery tribunal's interim award of 205 thousand million cubic feet volume of water by Karnataka to Tamil Nadu. The AIADMK made a big show by bringing cadres from across the state to express solidarity as she fasted for three days and two nights (eighty hours), lying on a cot brought from her house. The state health secretary issued regular medical bulletins. A caravan with a washroom was parked close to the fasting venue. Prime Minister Narasimha Rao finally sent the then Union Water Resources Minister V.C. Shukla to Chennai, with the assurance that a monitoring committee would be announced in good time. Jayalalithaa then sipped orange juice handed to her by Shukla. The committee was set up months later.

Although, the Congress-AIADMK alliance swept the Assembly polls in 1991, soon the relationship between the two parties began to sour. The author had witnessed how the two main groups in the Congress—led by G.K. Moopanar and Vazhapadi Ramamurthy—were quarrelling bitterly with each other, and, in the process, competing with each other in attacking Jaya, too. She began to believe that Prime Minister P.V. Narasimha Rao was supporting Moopanar in the attack, since he was perceived to be close to him. Moopanar was a tall Congress leader from Tamil Nadu and Congress prime ministers like Indira Gandhi, Rajiv Gandhi and Narasimha Rao used him for the party matters. Therefore, Jaya was suspicious of Rao's involvement.

Jaya was impulsive and wanted to resign from the chief ministership in 1992 in a huff when the media criticised her. Former President R. Venkataraman, who hailed from

Tamil Nadu, had retired and returned to Chennai. The then Tamil Nadu Governor Bhishma Narain Singh and R. Venkataraman were close friends, as both were ministers in the Indira Gandhi cabinet. Singh recounts the resignation drama in his own words: 'On the evening of August 5, 1992, I was somewhat free and decided to go to RV's (Venkataraman was called RV) house for a chat. I had a programme to visit Tirupathi, a temple town in Andhra Pradesh the following day. When I was sitting with RV, my ADC brought a slip around 7 pm. There was a call from Chief Minister Jayalalithaa that she wanted to meet me urgently. I sent her a slip mentioning that since my Tirupathi programme was a little doubtful, she might call on me the next morning. I had invited former minister Bindeswari Dubey for dinner that night. Dubey was in Chennai for a health check-up. I wanted to decide about my Tirupathi programme because I came to know of a bandh the next day, protesting against the sanction for some medical college by the Andhra Pradesh government.'[55] Singh adds, 'However, the ADC came back to me again saying that there was an SOS from the Chief Minister and that she wanted to meet me urgently. The matter was most serious. Then I left RV (Venkataraman), saying I had some urgent work and would meet him another day. RV had no clue as to what was going on. Half an hour later, when I arrived at Raj Bhavan, Jayalalithaa too arrived within five minutes and was seated in the drawing room. I found her quite flustered. I had never seen her in such a condition. I asked her what she would like to have—coffee or tea. She told me it could wait for the moment and she had something urgent to discuss. Then she threw the bombshell. She said that the state was quite stable and the government was doing well. She wanted to quit on health grounds. There were other competent people in her party who could take care of the administration. (She must have had Nedunchezhian, the permanent number two who could never make it to number one, in her mind.) I saw her clutching a letter in her hand and surmised that it must have been her resignation letter. However, I advised her to go and think it over calmly for the day and return next morning by 10 am. I also pointed out that I had not received or read her letter of resignation and that she was only telling me all this verbally.' The excuse for not accepting the resignation letter was that the Governor's staff had gone home, the office was closed, and he could not possibly retain the letter in his possession.

Singh pointed out to her as to how people had reposed their faith in her, and elected her with such a massive majority. Hence, she should think of the development of the state first. She apparently had regard for the Governor and listened to him carefully, after which she left quietly and did not return to Raj Bhavan the following day. That was the end of her resignation story.

The press got a whiff of the whole episode because reporters were waiting outside her house. Since she did not meet them or announce her resignation, the cat was out of the bag. It was obvious that ill health was a mere alibi for resignation, but the real problem lay elsewhere as Dr Swamy affirms: 'This was not the first time she had threatened to quit. Suddenly she would throw everything and go away. She is basically that kind of person and does not want anyone to know how she feels. She does not want people to have access to her. MGR was more accessible but she thinks people are after her money.'[56]

Jaya got along well with Singh. When the Centre decided to send Dr Chenna Reddy as his successor, she even spoke to the then Home Minister S.B. Chavan not to replace him. When Governor Dr Chenna Reddy was transferred from Rajasthan to Tamil Nadu in May 1993, she suspected that

Prime Minister Narasimha Rao had sent him to spy on her activities. By this time, there were differences between her and the local Congress leaders. Jayalalithaa erroneously began to think that the 1991 political victory was entirely due to her charisma. The Congress Party, on the other hand, felt it was due to the sympathy wave after the Rajiv Gandhi assassination. Also, she would not treat the local Congress leaders with any respect. Though initially she got along with Dr Reddy, the relationship soured quickly because Dr Reddy was equally arrogant and egoistic. Soon, the Governor and the Chief Minister could not bear to see each, other let alone talk.

Once when Prime Minister Narasimha Rao visited Chennai, the two held separate receptions for him at the airport. The relationship began to sour dramatically. Jaya decided to break up the political alliance unilaterally, in March 1993. The next two years saw constant bickering between Raj Bhavan and Poes Garden, her official residence. It was a clash of the titans. While Jaya was suspicious, Reddy thought that the Chief Minister was trying to undermine his authority as the Governor with her overbearing personality. This resulted in a stream of hostile press releases against each other. Tracing the souring of their relationship, *India Today* noted thus: 'First, Speaker Sedapatti Muthiah convened the Assembly without the Governor's customary New Year address. Then, the House passed a bill bringing all the universities under the control of the Chief Minister, thus depriving Reddy of his chancellorship. The insults have been piling up. According to a Raj Bhavan report, the Government has issued orders orally to all officials to boycott the Governor's functions, to prohibit the holding of his functions in government buildings and auditoriums and scale down the security on the Governor's route. Further, some ministers have made derogatory statements about Reddy.'[57]

Many of these misunderstandings between Reddy and Jayalalithaa stemmed from a confrontation between them in August 1993. *India Today* notes further that Reddy had summoned the Chief Minister to Raj Bhavan and criticised Jayalalithaa for her government's functioning. The Chief Minister, not used to being rebuked, left in a huff. That was the last time she stepped into the Raj Bhavan during Chenna Reddy's time.

Jaya tried to get rid of Dr Reddy. On a visit to New Delhi in September 1993, she called on the Prime Minister and urged him to withdraw Dr Reddy. She complained that he unnecessarily took more time to clear files. The next two years saw a constant clashing of egos between her and Governor Reddy.

It reached a peak in April 1995 when Dr Reddy gave the Janata Party president, Dr Subramanian Swamy the nod to prosecute Chief Minister Jayalalithaa on charges of corruption and criminal misconduct. The DMK-led Opposition was elated. For the Chief Minister, it was a major blow in the four years that she had been in power. The principal charges referred to Section 169 of the Indian Penal Code and Section 13 of the Prevention of Corruption Act. One was related to the purchase of a large plot of land purchased by Jaya Publications, owned by Jaya and Sasikala at a price far below the market rate. The other implicated her in abetting irregularities in a coal import deal in August 1993. The party, which worshipped its leader, suffered shock waves by the development. Even though corruption charges had been hurled at many people in public life, this was the first time that permission was granted for criminal prosecution of a sitting Chief Minister.

As *Frontline* magazine notes in its 5 May 1995 issue: 'The Jayalalithaa regime of 1991-96 also used brutal physical violence against the state Governor, its political opponents, advocates, an IAS officer, a Vice Chancellor, the then Chief Election Commissioner, and its own legislators. The AIADMK's cult of violence first came into the open on August 14, 1991, within three months of its coming to power, when armed men stormed the office of *Tharasu*, a Tamil magazine, and stabbed two of its employees to death. The next day, during an Independence Day party, even as Governor Bhishma Narain Singh and Jayalalithaa were chatting on the lawns of Raj Bhavan, women AIADMK MLAs gheraoed the then Union Minister of state for Commerce P. Chidambaram to protest against the Union government's decision to refer the Cauvery dispute to the Supreme Court.' Acid was thrown on IAS officer V.S. Chandralekha on 19 May 1992, when she was the Commissioner of Tamil Nadu Archives and Historical Research. She received severe burns on her face, neck and hands. Though it was made out that her estranged husband was the mastermind behind the attack, the public perception was different. The attack, it was believed, was because of her objection to the low price at which the disinvestment in the chemicals giant Southern Petrochemicals Industries Corporation (SPIC) was ordered by the Chief Minister just a few days before the attack.

On 21 July 1994, as advocate K.M. Vijayan stepped out of his house to go to the airport, four men beat him up with clubs. Vijayan suffered multiple fractures on his legs. As Nirupama Subramanian writes in *India Today* on 5 October 1994, 'Recently, he was attacked by goondas outside his house in east Madras just as he was about to leave for Delhi, this time to petition for a stay order on the implementation of the Tamil Nadu 69 per cent Reservations Act. The assault was so severe that it broke two bones in his right arm, caused multiple fractures in his left leg and confined him to bed for at least three months. Four men "surrendered" some days after the attack. Their identities were not made public. So flimsy was the case made out by the police against them that the High Court granted them bail immediately. On the direction of the Supreme Court, the case was handed over to the CBI last month.'

Nirupama Subramanian adds: 'The attack has only further strengthened the belief that it is now getting increasingly dangerous for the state's citizens to tread on political corns. Beginning with the murder of two employees of the Tamil weekly, *Tharasu*, in August 1991 in which a Home Secretary of the Karunanidhi regime was implicated, matters have gone from bad to worse. It was clear that Jaya was intolerant about criticisms and punished those whom she thought crossed her road. Drunk by her power and arrogance, she resorted to this each time someone did something against the interests of the Chief Minister or her party. She did not spare her political enemies or any one who crossed her path.'

Her first five-year term was completed amidst several avoidable controversies. It was a mixed bag of successes and setbacks. Jayalalithaa frittered away the immense goodwill she acquired in the initial days of her first term. Known as the youngest Chief Minister of the state, who drew a token salary of Re 1, her stint is still being remembered for various social welfare programmes, which were later, recreated in other states.

As the 1996 Assembly elections came closer, Jaya realised the need for alliance and once again telephoned Prime Minister P.V. Narasimha Rao, seeking an alliance with the Congress. She knew that it was arithmetic, more than chemistry, which was needed for a poll victory. Local Congress leaders, including G.K. Moopanar and P. Chidambaram, were against the tie-up with the AIADMK because they were worried about the corrupt image of the Jayalalithaa government. This section, led by Moopanar, believed that the Congress would not do well if it aligned with the AIADMK. They also believed that the anti incumbency factor was against Jayalalithaa. They wanted the Congress to align with the DMK whose chief, Karunanidhi, was a friend of Moopanar.

The DMK, looking for an opportunity to strengthen itself, had stretched out a friendly hand to the Congress. The DMK chief had also deputed a person of his confidence to camp in Delhi to try for the tie-up. Guhan, a retired IAS officer and Karunanidhi's close adviser, was sent to Delhi to talk to the Congress leaders. However, he did not succeed as the Congress Working Committee (CWC) decided to go with the AIADMK.

Political parties had, over the years, tried to capitalise the mass appeal of the Tamil superstar Rajnikant. Prime Minister Rao also met with matinee idol Rajnikant, and after two or three meetings, it was evident that he was not willing to jump into politics, and would only advise his fan clubs. The Congress Working Committee decided to let the alliance with AIADMK be revived. Then came the split in the Tamil Nadu Congress. Moopanar, Chidambaram, Arunachalam, Jayanthi Natarajan and other leaders belonging to the Moopanar faction left the Congress and launched a regional party, Tamizhaga Maanila Congress (TMC). Karunanidhi joined with the Tamizhaga Maanila Congress, and the DMK front emerged successful. Moopanar also had a stake at the Centre when the United Front formed the coalition government with Deve Gowda as the Prime Minister. It was a coalition of small regional parties, which had nothing in common and they came together for the sake of power. The DMK and the TMC both bagged hefty portfolios at the Centre.

Governor Dr Chenna Reddy continued to be hostile to Jaya. When this author went to Chennai to cover the 1996 general and Assembly elections, Dr Reddy revealed in detail Jaya's alleged acts of omission and commission (corruption was a major plank). He indicated that his preference was for the Congress–DMK alliance.

Narasimha Rao was one person who had a long political alliance with Jayalalithaa, and also witnessed the highs and lows of the alliance. This relationship had several angularities, yet it continued. He had his elucidation on different aspects of their alliance and other issues that cropped up during 1991–96. Beginning with the open show of annoyance, which Jayalalithaa gave vent to, Rao explained: 'I had no idea whether she was annoyed with me, and why. Regarding Dr Chenna Reddy, the reasons for his shift, at his own request, from Rajasthan, lay entirely in Rajasthan and had nothing to do with Tamil Nadu. Indeed, I did the customary consultation with Jayalalithaaji and she agreed. There was not the slightest intention on my part to cause any difficulty to her. I did not even know that she felt that way, since there was no conceivable reason known to me for such a feeling.'[58]

Though their relationship was cordial in his view, circumstances shifted rapidly, as he noted the strained relations between Tamil Nadu Congressmen and AIADMK ministers and workers. To some extent, this was inherent in the situation at the state level, where the two parties were rivals and their coming together also had the built-in danger of yielding the opposition ground to the DMK. He also knew that personal attacks on Jayalalithaa by some local Congress leaders were more serious, because the identity between her and her party was complete; they were almost indistinguishable. So it was not quite realistic to expect the relations between the Congress and the AIADMK inter se,

A rare picture of Jayalalithaa in the Bishop Cotton School in Bangalore as a child.
(Photo Credit : Courtesy egk and son studio bangalore (only digital copy))

M.G.Ramachandran and his heroine Jayalalithaa in the Tamil film Maattukara Velan, a super hit. (Photo Credit : The Hindu)

One of the rare photographs of Jayalalithaa soon after she joined the Party in 1982, interacting with the then labour minister Raghavanandam during the Independence Day celebrations at Fort St George. (Photo Credit : The Hindu(V. Ramamurthi))

Jayalalithaa at the party conference with MGR. (Photo Credit : The Hindu)

A rare picture of MGR with his wife Janaki on his left and Jayalalithaa on his right.

Rajiv Gandhi and Jayalalithaa waving to the crowds. (Photo Credit : The Hindu)

Jayalalalithaa trying to claim the legacy of MGR when his body was being taken on a gun carriage in December 1987. (Photo Credit : The Hindu)

Jayalalithaa being pulled down from the gun carriage, carrying MGR's body. (Photo Credit : The Hindu)

Jayalalithaa sworn in as the first Tamil Nadu chief minister by Governor Bhishma Narain Singh. (Photo Credit : The Hindu)

Sasikala giving a holy bath to Jayalalithaa when they went to participate in the Kumbakonam Mahamagam.
(Photo Credit : Special arrangement)

Jayalalithaa and Sasikala wearing identical sarees and jewellery before Jaya's foster son's wedding.

Jayalalithaa with the bride and groom at her foster son Sudhakaran's wedding. (Photo Credit : The Hindu)

Jayalalithaa with Sasikala at the reception held for her foster son Sudhakaran's wedding. (Photo Credit : The Hindu)

Jayalalithaa and Sonia Gandhi shaking hands at the famous tea party, which brought down the Vajpayee government in 1999. (Photo Credit : Delhi News Photos (sarswathi s))

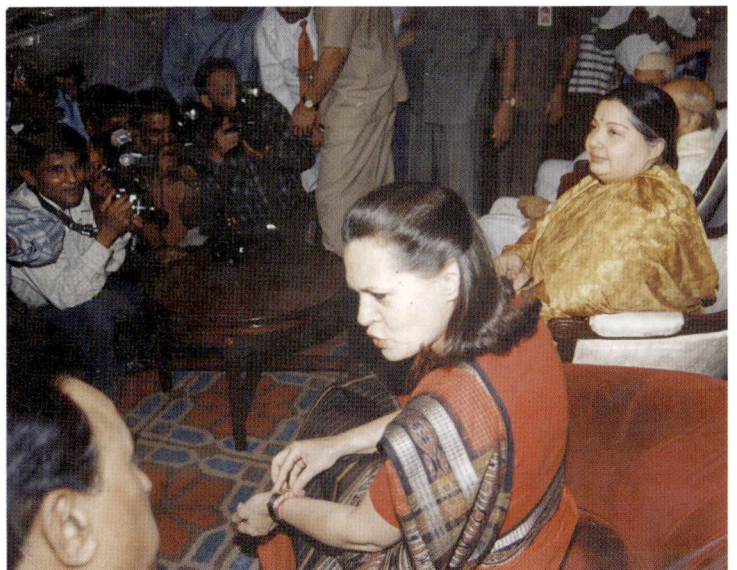

Jayalalithaa, Sonia Gandhi and Dr Subramanian Swamy addressing the press after the tea party in 1999. (Photo Credit : The Hindu)

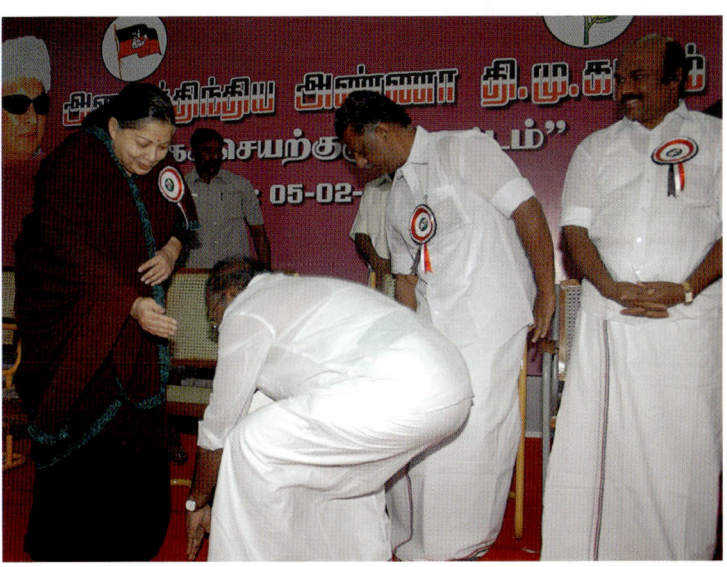

Madhusudan, Party's elected presidium chairman touching the feet of Jayalalithaa. (Photo Credit : The Hindu)

Jayalalithaa during her campaign addressing the voters from her specially built van.
(Photo Credit : The Hindu)

Jayalalalithaa waving to her balcony audience showing the victory sign .
(Photo Credit : The Hindu)

A victorious Jayalalithaa interacting with her party workers after her spectacular win in 2001. (Photo Credit : The Hindu)

Jayalalithaa introducing the first time MLA Pannerselvam as her puppet Chief Minister when she was disqualified in 2001.
(Photo Credit : Vino John (digital image))

Jayalalithaa, Sasikala and Pannerselvam at the swearing in ceremony in Raj Bhavan in 2001. (Photo Credit : K.Gajendran)

Jayalalithaa during her campaign-addressing voters. (Photo Credit : The Hindu)

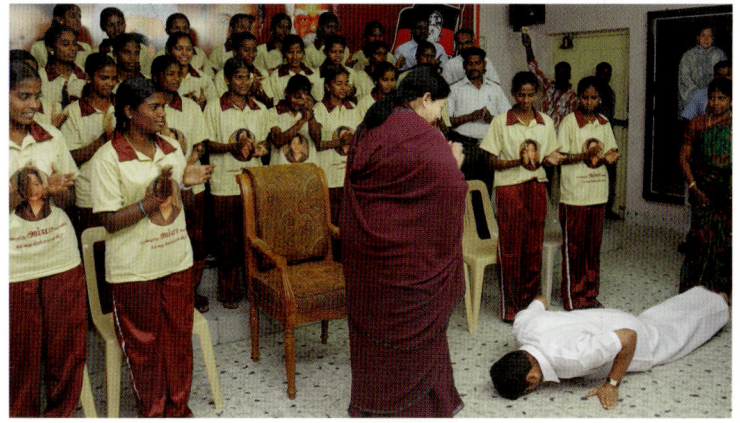

An AIADMK leader prostrating before Jayalalithaa. (Photo Credit : The Hindu)

O. Pannerselvam, falling at the feet of Jayalalithaa. (Photo Credit : The Hindu)

Jayalalithaa sitting in her car during her drive to the Secretariat greeting her workers with folded hands. (Photo Credit : The Hindu)

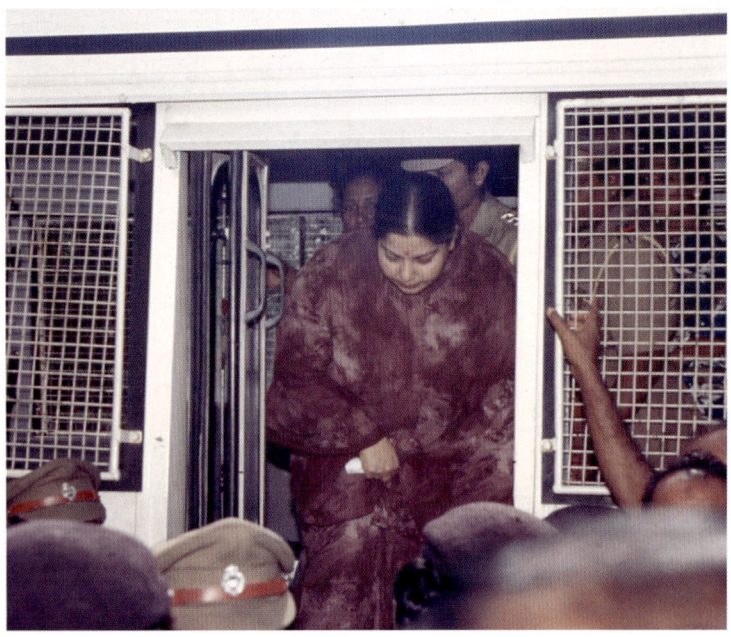

Jayalalithaa brought from her prison in Bangalore. (Photo Credit : The Hindu)

Jayalalithaa after her acquittal in Bangalore. (Photo Credit : The Hindu)

Jayalalithaa paying tribute to her mentor MGR ahead of her swearing in ceremony after she was acquitted . (Photo Credit : M_Prabhu)

AIADMK workers rejoicing Jayalalithaa's acquittal by beating the drums.
(Photo Credit : The Hindu)

AIADMK workers distributing laddus in Bangalore after the Karnataka High Court acquitted Jayalalithaa in 2015. (Photo Credit : M. Periasamy)

The funeral procession of Jayalalithaa on December 6, 2016.
(Photo Credit : G_Sribharath)

Prime Minister Narendra Modi and Governor C. Vidyasagar Rao paying tribute to Jayalalithaa during the funeral procession. (Photo Credit : The Hindu)

Sasikala going to jail on February 15, 2017 after she was convicted.
(Photo Credit : The Hindu)

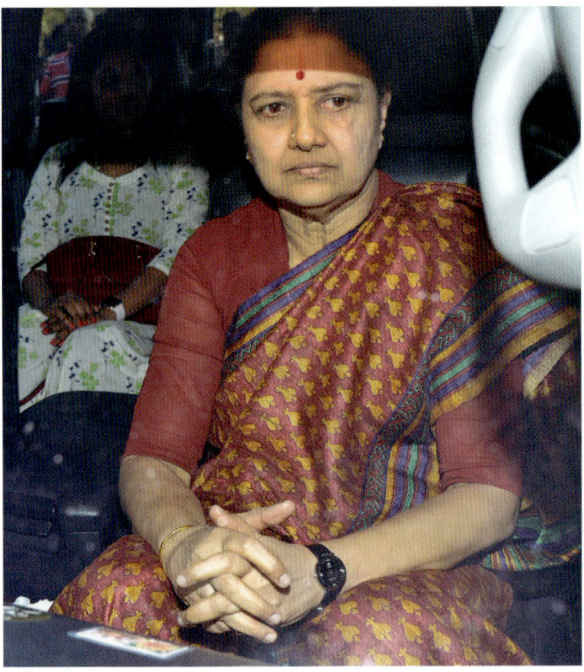

Sasikala on her way to Parapana Agraharam jail after she was convicted.
(Photo Credit : The Hindu)

to become really cordial at the state level. There could only be a working relationship. 'But at the Central level, Rajiv Gandhi and later, myself found it mutually advantageous to forge and retain our alliance. To the best of my conscience and knowledge, my dealings with the Chief Ministers were fair and just. The Prime Minister's job also includes, in my view and previous experience in government, putting up with occasional tirades from Chief Ministers on a number of issues—and sometimes even on non-issues. Anti-Centre consensus is seen as easier to forge and manage at the state level and to some extent relieves local pressures. I have operated at both ends and have a fairly accurate idea of the situations faced at both. This is part of the Constitutional scenario we all have to live with. Before the 1996 elections, the CWC had a marathon meeting on Tamil Nadu, at which the state Congress leaders pleaded their case thoroughly. I did not figure anywhere in the discussion personally, since I knew the extreme delicacy of the matter and the options— rather the lack of options—available. The CWC's decision to go along with the AIADMK was unanimous, categorical and final. Under the circumstances, the emergence of a new party could only have been a surprise. I shall leave it at that. From all reports, Ms Jayalalithaa cooperated wholeheartedly with the Congress candidates. She did not ask for any financial assistance from me.'[59]

The 1996 Assembly election results eventually showed that Jaya was not a goddess anymore when people rejected her. She naively assumed that no matter what, people would elect her again, which was proved wrong. The 1996 poll results came as a severe blow to Jayalalithaa who thought she could remain in power forever, even though she was the first Chief Minister to complete the full term in the state. She did little to change the perception that she was heading a corrupt administration. While she was enthusiastic to do something for the people, soon this waned and her hunger for power was exposed. When Jayalalithaa became Tamil Nadu Chief Minister in 1991, one of her first acts was to introduce the Cradle Baby scheme, meant to reduce female infanticide, and to help the poor parents to take care of their daughters, in Salem district. The scheme helped the parents to leave unwanted female babies in the white, painted cradles kept outside the district's 115 clinics. This was a successful welfare scheme, which brought her kudos. Jaya was also the first to reserve 30 per cent police jobs for women and establish all-women police stations. She also kick-started several notable public health programmes, including the formation of state-run pharmaceutical companies and distribution of medicine. But as she was nearing the end of her first term, she did not introduce any more such welfare schemes. People started talking about her corruption and not about any welfare schemes. This was evident from the way people did not vote for her. 'She filed cases against anyone who reported on her supposedly poor health, forcing on one instance the web portal Rediff to take down an article. More than a dozen cases were filed against the *Times of India*, *The Hindu*, Tamil newspaper *Dinamalar*, compelling the Supreme Court to rebuke the state government and accuse it of "throttling democracy".[60] The Congress got a beating at the state level as well as at the national level, while the DMK-TMC combine came out successful in Tamil Nadu. Jayalalithaa was isolated, with no support from either the Centre or the state.

It was not surprising that Jaya and her party lost miserably in the 1996 Assembly polls. She was defeated even in her home constituency, Bargur, which was much more humiliating to her. All her seventeen ministers lost the elections and the Congress candidates were defeated in all the sixty-six seats they contested. The DMK, the

TMC, the Communist Party of India (CPI) and two other small parties contested as allies against the AIADMK. The arithmetic could not go wrong. The DMK won 172 out of 176 seats it contested, and the TMC thirty-nine out of the forty seats it contested.

Jayalalithaa's bête noire Karunanidhi became the next Chief Minister, in 1996, rubbing salt into her wounds. He won on the anti-Jayalalithaa wave. His arithmetic did the rest of the magic.

Soon after he took over, Karunanidhi foisted forty-six cases under the Prevention of Corruption Act, which was applicable to public servants, against Jayalalithaa, her erstwhile ministers and some bureaucrats. Of these cases, nine were filed against Jayalalithaa. She and Sasikala were arrested and put behind bars. Disproportionate assets were discovered during a CBI raid at her residence. Jaya fought back bravely, using a battery of lawyers to defend herself. She was fighting Karunanidhi politically and did not miss a single occasion to tell people that the cases against her were politically motivated. 'Wait for the outcome of cases in court. If I say anything, it will amount to contempt of court. I will only say that all the cases are politically motivated. We will stand vindicated in the end,' she maintained all through.[61]

So why did Jaya lose? She had acquired a bad image and lost mostly because of that, notes Moopanar: 'Again her politics was only vis-à-vis the DMK and she had no role to play for her larger constituency. Still she could not digest the fact that the people of Tamil Nadu could throw her out the way they did. She was terribly upset. She actually blamed the people for letting her down and felt she had wasted her life.'[62] Dr Swamy adds, 'Jaya told me that she made many mistakes, but she made mistakes again.'

The Tamil Nadu voters have alternated between the DMK and the AIADMK since 1967. The Congress, which lost power in that year, had simply been riding piggyback on either of the Dravidian parties since then. Both have had around 30 per cent committed voters. Jaya's five-year rule resulted in an increase in the anti-establishment vote. The split in the Congress helped the TMC-DMK combine. The last two years from 1994 saw corruption charges on the rise. She was accused of being inaccessible, in the grip of her associate Sasikala, and harassing the media by foisting libel suits against journalists. The initial goodwill she enjoyed with the media evaporated soon. By the time she finished her first term her popularity nose-dived. The sympathy wave following the Rajiv Gandhi assassination had also disappeared as had internal quarrels within the local Congress that affected the party. In the five years of her rule, the AIADMK general council met only once. Jayalalithaa would visit the party office once or twice a year, and that too on ceremonial occasions. This was in sharp contrast to MGR's style of functioning, who met party men every day in order to get a feedback on the party and the government. In short, she lost contact with the cadres as well as the people.

Moreover, Jayalalithaa did nothing to fight the perception battle: One can't deny that politics is perception. During her first term, rumours were rife that Jayalalithaa and Sasikala were scouting for prime property and land, and house owners were petrified fearing that Sasikala might be eyeing their property. Traffic was stalled for hours every time her convoy left her home, putting the public to inconvenience. Super star Rajnikant was one of those affected by the traffic stalling. *The Telegraph* reports that once he was stopped when Jaya's motorcade was passing through. 'He stepped out of the car, walked towards a "box shop", bought a packet of 555, leaned against a lamppost and lit a cigarette. Within seconds, people were making a "beeline" for the screen star who seemed to have appeared from nowhere. Dr Radhakrishan Road soon became an "umbrella of human heads". Aware that Jayalalithaa's motorcade was minutes away, the police officer in-charge of the area's traffic rushed towards Rajnikant and requested him to move away. "Sir," the actor replied. "I am waiting for her to pass. I don't mind waiting."[63]

To top it all, the vulgar show of wealth and power in performing the marriage of her adopted son also did not go down well with the public. The bride was the grand daughter of matinee idol Sivaji Ganesan. The groom was Sasikala's nephew, Sudhakaran. At least 12,000 guests sat down for a lavish dinner prepared by 3,000 cooks at the wedding. The *New York Times* described the wedding thus: 'One of India's leading film set designers was summoned to make the whole avenues in central Madras a tableau of Tamil mythology. For miles between Jayalalithaa's official residence (Poes Garden) and the wedding site, streets were decorated with pillared castles decorated with Grecian statues and gilded lions. Shrines were erected with icons like images of Jayalalithaa in place of Hindu gods. Fountains played and the turmoil of daily street life was hidden by from the view by walls of banana leaves.'[64] All these marred her image as a well-meaning person who was eager to do good for the people. There was public outcry when her arrest in 1996 was followed by the seizure of 29 kilos of gold and diamond studded jewellery, more than 10,000 sarees and 750 pairs of shoes from her Poes Garden residence. Her rout was complete as she lost her own constituency to an unknown tea vendor.

Quite on the contrary, *Frontline* magazine said that 'in the last five years (1991-1996) 'her [Jayalalithaa] government acquired a unique reputation among all state governments in India without exception for unbridled corruption, acts of high-handedness, mind-boggling extravagance and vulgarity as a new public virtue. She travelled in thousand-car convoys. Sycophancy stooped to new lows, literally: Ministers and MLAs—some of whom were much her senior—prostrated before her in public. An opulent cut-out culture flourished; giant cardboard representations of the caped Chief Minister towered over street corners (and occasionally came crashing down on account of natural causes). Whenever she stepped out of her high-security residence to take part in a function, her cut-outs came up on either side of the road for kilometres.'[65]

During her first term, she rode the liberalisation wave launched in 1991 by Narasimha Rao as the economy of the country did well and people were happy, although there were complaints that it lacked a human face. Taking advantage of the reform process, Jaya opened up the state's economy by jumping into the bandwagon. Jaya propelled the already present initial enabling conditions for economic growth in the state further during 1991-96. The American auto major Ford Motor Company's major foray in 1995 with its first passenger car facility in India at Maraimalainagar, 45 km South of Chennai, under the first Jayalalithaa regime, was the big trigger point. This was soon followed by another big ticket investment by Korean car maker Hyundai in 1996, setting up its plant near Sriperumbudur (near Chennai).

After she lost the 1996 Assembly elections, Jaya once again broke up with the Congress. Both Rao and Jayalalithaa got embroiled in several court cases. The AIADMK was isolated in the state and also at the Centre. But undaunted, Jayalalithaa went ahead with her plan and started working for the next elections, which came in 1998 (Lok Sabha polls) when the Congress Party pulled down the United Front government on the issue of the Jain Commission report. The Commission pointed a finger at the DMK involvement in the Rajiv Gandhi assassination. Prime Minister I.K. Gujral refused to sack the DMK ministers in his cabinet as demanded by the Congress President Sitaram Kesri. Jaya thought that it was better to join hands with a national party, and hence aligned with the BJP for the 1998 Lok Sabha polls. Much later, eyeing the 2014 Lok Sabha polls, it was the BJP leader L.K. Advani who termed the AIADMK as the 'natural ally'. He said the cooperation extended by the AIADMK chief Jayalalithaa and her party made it feel AIADMK is our 'natural ally,' while speaking at the anniversary celebrations of the Tamil weekly *Thuglak* in 2012. Advani said though the Tamil Nadu Chief Minister was not part of the National Democratic Alliance (NDA) group, there was an understanding with the southern party in Parliament. In 1998, the alliance clicked and the AIADMK won a handsome number of twenty-seven out of the thirty-nine seats, giving a solid support to the BJP-led Vajpayee government, which came to power with twenty-four partners. For the BJP, the AIADMK contingent was important. Jaya became a powerful force at the Central level. She kept Vajpayee waiting for his swearing-in ceremony, and would not send her party's letter of support to the President. Ultimately, she gave clearance to Kumar (her minister in the Central Government) on the fourth night to hand over the letter to the President. Throughout the 13-month period, until she finally pulled down the Vajpayee government in 1999, there were pinpricks from her sometimes for induction of more ministers or demand for better portfolios. Her party members became Central ministers but her main aim was to get out of the corruption cases.

Jana Krishnamurthy was quite forthright when he observed: 'AIADMK's relationship with the BJP was never deep-rooted. We also knew fully well the difficulties we may be facing when we went for a tie-up with Jayalalithaa. She too must have felt that she may not be able to get along with the BJP for long and that BJP leadership will not be pliable. We were also ready from the beginning to break off the relationship but we would not have done it on our own.'[66]

The relationship with the BJP began to sour within a year, with Jayalalithaa demanding many things, and the Prime Minister was not willing to oblige. She expected that the Centre would get her out of her court cases, which did not happen. The break-up with the BJP was inevitable and it came in the form of a tea party and it was not just a storm in the teacup, as it led to the fall of the Vajpayee government in thirteen months. At a tea party hosted by Dr Swamy, Congress President Sonia Gandhi and Jayalalithaa sipped tea together and plotted against Vajpayee. The tea party drew international attention as the *New York Times* noted, 'The two women spent less than ten minutes together, drinking tea. But the mere fact of their public chat made the front pages. "We are old friends," Mrs Gandhi said, which was news in itself. Conjecture began about a budding alliance.'[67] Eyebrows were raised because the Congress and the AIADMK were not on good terms and the vibes were cold between the two women leaders.

Dr Swamy, who was the main player in the whole drama, says, 'It was Jaya's idea. I had been telling her from day one, "Don't go with the BJP". She went with them. I told her they would cut you out afterwards. She later on said that I was right but she wanted to withdraw. I told her, "First you create an atmosphere and build bridges with the Congress and other parties." She said that Sonia would not even come to her. That was in July 1998. I made them talk to each other on my cellular phone. In the first week of March 1999, she rang me up and told me, "I am coming to Delhi. You have to give a tea party." I said, "You've already been invited by the BJP for a tea party." Vijay Goel, who was a minister in Vajpayee's cabinet, hosted that tea party which was attended by Prime Minister Vajpayee. She told me, "You arrange for a tea party and if Sonia comes over, we will work on the fall of the government." Even then I told her, "Remember this is your ace of trumps; so don't use it unless you have something else as the alternative". She came and we had the tea party and Jayalalithaa called it "a political earthquake." She was carried away. Then I told her, "let us wait for some time". The party was on March 29 and by April 12, she announced at the airport she was going to Delhi and would not come back until a new government came to power. She came here and nobody was willing to talk to her because they said she was still with the BJP and she was only bargaining. They said, "Withdraw first." I told her that they would all be saying that, but I would not advise so. Then she went and met Sonia and something happened there.'[68] Soon afterwards, Vajpayee lost his government by one vote when Jaya pulled down the government.

Looking back, it may not be out of place to point out here that whatever the players themselves might say, one fact scored over all else, that the 1999 pull-down drama was free-for-all wherein everyone tried to outwit everyone else. The first hopeful—and very promising—symptom appeared in the form of Jayalalithaa's dissatisfaction with Vajpayee's Central Government. Instantly, a consensus to topple the BJP government emerged. Several opposition parties were involved in this enterprise, but each had its own agenda, distinct from the other. Sonia Gandhi's ambition suddenly soared very high. In the ensuing days, she seemed to have taken both Dr Subramanian Swamy and Jayalalithaa for a ride. While Jayalalithaa used Dr Swamy, the Marxist leader Surjit Singh took Sonia Gandhi on a merry-go-round; Mulayam Singh might have made half a promise to

Surjit Singh. It was thus a game of wits all round. As a result, many experts felt that Sonia Gandhi's high ambition and haste to become the Prime Minister were fully exposed and she fell a notch in the estimation of the people. But more than anyone else, Jayalalithaa lost her strong bargaining position. She was seen as the immediate cause that led to the Lok Sabha elections of 1999, only to find, to her utter discomfiture, that the DMK had become a partner in the BJP-led National Democratic Alliance, meanwhile. Prior to that, the DMK supported the Vajpayee government in the confidence motion in 1999 when Jayalalithaa pulled down his government. It is common knowledge that the two Dravidian parties cannot support the same party at the national or state level because of their enmity. She found herself nowhere and without friends because she fell out even with the Congress.

It is no secret that Jaya was ambitious and wanted to become deputy Chief Minister even while MGR was alive. Dr Swamy claims that MGR knew of her ambition. 'Oh yes, Jaya was ambitious. She understood politics and she breathed politics. That arrogance had existed from the beginning. Before MGR died he wanted to get rid of her. He came to know of a letter written by her to Rajiv Gandhi asking him to make her the deputy Chief Minister. The then Home Minister, Buta Singh, gave the letter to him.'[69]

However, Jaya liked to project an image that she was not after power. The Indian public does not like leaders who are power hungry. She claimed that she spurned Prime Minister Vajpayee's offer to become the Defence Minister. 'That shows I am not power-crazy or power-hungry. I was offered the post of Defence Minister but I refused it,' she countered. Thus, there are two versions about her ambition. In actual practice, she was ambitious. Dr Swamy points out: 'For me, it was a full adventure.

I had to do only one thing—to pull down the Vajpayee government. But for Jaya it was sad. If she had left it to me I would have done it better. But once we brought down the government, she said Dinakaran (AIADMK MP and Sasikala's nephew) and herself would handle it. They made a mess of things. As for her Prime Ministerial ambitions, she never told me, but at one stage she did tell Mulayam Singh that he should support her. West Bengal Chief Minister Jyoti Basu told me that when she had come and tried to persuade him to accept Prime Ministership, he said jokingly, "You are there." He said she had taken it seriously and she went and told Mulayam. He asked me to correct her impression, since he had not meant it seriously. But I had no heart to tell her.'[70]

Before the 2014 Lok Sabha polls, when it was expected that there could be a coalition government, Jayalalithaa was getting ready to stake her claim for the Prime Minister's post in case the smaller parties came together to form a government at the Centre. Unfortunately for her, the BJP got a majority on its own and Narendra Modi became the Prime Minister.

JAYA: THE WOMAN WITH AN IRON WILL

What really sustained Jaya—the woman with an iron will? Her unflagging spirit, the unrelenting perseverance and the courage to hit back despite all odds helped her politically. Even as more and more legal cases piled up, she did not give up her fight. Also, the people had not given her up totally, going by her vote bank in 1998 and 1999, and the subsequent elections. Jayalalithaa had often declared in public that she would become the Chief Minister again. She did not have to wait for long. Her claim was generally ignored with some derision. It was not taken seriously, since it could not be, with the dice massively loaded against her for some years. By 2001, she got her arithmetic correct. The AIADMK, along with the TMC, Congress, the Left parties and others swept the 2001 Assembly polls, demolishing the DMK and NDA alliance.

Senior columnist T.V.R. Shenoy makes an astute observation: 'Why did Jaya win a second term? There are two aspects to that. In India, there is a simple theory that a woman cannot be corrupt. What will she do with the money? May be buy jewellery and clothes. For a man it is different—he may spend it on many other things. Indians as a mass accept moral issues. They had defeated Jaya but they may not accept the legal side. This is not a permanent punishment. People may feel that "we have punished her enough." Politics is not an element of legality. It is an element of morality. In the case of Indira Gandhi also, they tried to fix her through Shaw Commission and she bounced back. People felt that she had been punished enough.'[71]

Her re-ascension to power in 2001 had several facets to it: political, anti-incumbency, public sympathy, image-based, adroit management, DMK blunders, and last but not the least, legal and constitutional; and, of course, luck! The DMK lost power. Jayalalithaa shrewdly built a rag-tag coalition with a number of smaller parties and the Left parties, which brought her the magic number. The coalition won 197 of the 234 seats, the AIADMK winning 132 of those.

The *New York Times* described her victory like this: 'Jayalalithaa Jayaram, a flamboyant politician convicted six months ago on corruption charges, led an alliance of parties to a landslide victory in elections this week in Tamil Nadu, taking the state with heavy support from women and rural poor.'[72]

Politically, it had been proven in the Lok Sabha elections of 1998 and 1999, that despite the legal cases, her party managed to retain its vote share more or less. It was thus inevitable that in the Assembly elections, too, this position should be reflected. It was also noteworthy that Jayalalithaa's charisma was in a way the reflection of the great MGR, apart from her own. People recognised that she was wearing MGR's mantle and leading the campaign with his photograph, so they found it difficult to vote it down. Yes, they had done so in 1996, to demonstrate that no one was indispensable and when people don't like a leader's ways, they unhesitatingly throw him or her out. Having shown that, there was no need to repeat the trouncing in subsequent elections. And this was clearly proven in the Lok Sabha polls.

Jaya's surprise win in 2001 heralded the beginning of a very different kind of regime. She was no longer referred to as 'JJ' or 'Puratchi Thalaivi'. She became Amma: mother. In Indian politics, leaders have always tried to connect with the people by calling themselves as one of their relatives. For instance, Mahatma Gandhi was called 'Bapu' or father; Nehru was 'Chacha' or uncle; Mayawati is 'Behenji' or sister; Mamata Banerjee is 'Didi' or elder sister; Annadurai was 'Anna' or elder brother; and Indira Gandhi was 'Indiramma' or mother Indira, and so on. Therefore, it was not surprising that Jaya chose to become 'Amma' to her people. She wanted to be the mother to her voters, which would appeal to people of all castes and creeds. She appeared to be remorseful without apologising for the excesses during her first term. Instead, she thought of welfare schemes and freebees in the form of food, education and shelter.

For a considerable length of time, the DMK's reputation had been sliding. It was also true that Karunanidhi's regime this time was cleaner than it had been in the earlier stints. Yet, there was a peculiar fatigue about a party, which remained in power for long. The various cases slapped on Jayalalithaa at DMK's instance definitely became counter-productive—especially from the improper personal treatment she was reported to have received in jail. Jaya recalled with a shudder: 'That was I think the worst moment of my life. It was a miserable situation. Among all the prisons in Tamil Nadu, the Madras Central Prison is the worst. It is the most unhygienic, dirtiest prison imaginable. And the place where I was kept was a condemned building. This was reopened in my honour. You must have seen of these old English movies where they show these medieval dungeons. It was exactly like that. A dark dungeon, it had not been swept or cleaned for years probably, there were cobwebs everywhere, growth of fungus everywhere and all kinds of vermin crawling all over the place. You could have conducted a zoology class there. There were big rats, sewer rats, bandicoots, I had to sit or lie down on the bare floor, and Madras Central Prison is situated bang on the Cooum River, which is nothing but an open sewer. It was stinking to high hell. I stayed there for a month.'[73] Details of her prison days came out later. This vendetta politics shocked the public. The bumper crop of criminal cases against Jayalalithaa over the past several years had its own lessons for all. Some had already resulted in conviction and sentence, while others were pending. Whatever their status, if the motive behind them, even partly, had been to block Jaya's return to political prominence, her detractors had failed in this attempt. The masses had either not believed in the charges levelled against Amma, or believed them to be mala fide. So they ignored them while voting. And Jayalalithaa, as a result, ruled Tamil Nadu in style. People contemplated between the two Dravidian parties and chose the AIADMK.

Even when there are two main political parties, other parties of varying sizes and popularity often tilt the scales. A massive vote for a single party is becoming less and less frequent, as the political process passes through new phases and newer generations. In the present instance, the Congress, the TMC, the Pattali Makkal Katchi (PMK), the MDMK, the Communists, etc., seem to have added up considerably to the AIADMK, both in vote share and even more in general morale and acceptability. Appearances became right for the AIADMK, and wrong for the DMK, which, in the earlier elections, had mobilised those parties on its side. Jayalalithaa's alliance management was obviously superior and more timely, and this paid rich dividends. The DMK goofed up in this regard, as its own internal factors seem to have played a major role in its alienation.

It is interesting to investigate how the law and the Constitution stood in regard to Jayalalithaa's political position. At the surface level, the whole thing seemed outrageous to the layman. There were several questions like how can one explain a person convicted and sentenced to three-year imprisonment becoming the Chief Minister again; or whoever heard of such a monstrosity; and what is India coming to; these were the reaction from her detractors. But the legal process followed its own path. An odd anomaly raises eyebrows once in a while; at the same time, the rule of law had a sound logic. From a layman's standpoint, the following features may be briefly enumerated with regard to this remarkable case of 'prison to throne'. Jayalalithaa, in one case, was convicted and sentenced to three years' imprisonment. She appealed to the High Court and the verdict was kept under suspension, pending disposal of the appeal. As per the Representation of People's Act, any person sentenced to more than two years' imprisonment cannot contest in any election. Jayalalithaa filed her nomination from four Assembly constituencies. However, the Election Commission of India had, in 1997, sent executive instructions to all the Returning Officers to reject the nomination papers of all candidates convicted and sentenced.

The Supreme Court of India has held in several cases that conviction in the trial court is not finality by itself. It becomes final only as per the final verdict of the highest court after disposal of the appeals. In view of this, it appears that the Election Commission's order in 1997 was in contravention of the law as enunciated by the Supreme Court. However, in obedience to the Election Commission's orders, the returning officers rejected the nomination papers; so Jayalalithaa did not contest. Meanwhile, her party returned in the Assembly polls with a huge majority and recommended to the Governor to appoint Jayalalithaa as the Chief Minister. Thus, Jayalalithaa's ascendancy to Chief Ministership opened up several vistas for scanning—including, whether the people have now become capable of instinctively 'smelling' politically motivated cases, where the course of the law is sought to be misused for settling political scores. It is also a moot question whether the people stick to only one criterion in choosing their candidates, or go by their own general appraisal of what they expect from their representatives? Whatever the facts in the cases (which only the court will decide), people's perceptions have definitely undergone a sea change in sophistication and truculence over the decades.

A triumphant Jayalalithaa began ruling despite the uncertainty about her future, in 2001. Meanwhile a Public Interest Litigation (PIL) was filed in the Supreme Court questioning the legality of her holding the post of the Chief Minister using a provision. She became Chief Minister without being a legislator. When Jaya was chosen as the AIADMK legislature party leader, Governor Fatima Beevi, who was a former Supreme Court judge, appointed her without any questions, going by the convention that anyone chosen by the legislature party with the magic number should be given a chance. Jaya had to step down following the Supreme Court verdict that a convicted person could not be sworn in. This order came on the morning of 21 September 2001.

Jaya got to know about her disqualification around 11.30 a.m. She called her Chief Secretary P. Shankar and asked if she had to resign. After checking up the legal position, he informed her that she should do so. She immediately made arrangements to call a legislature party meeting (to elect a new Chief Minister) after meeting the Governor, C. Rangarajan, at 1 p.m. The Governor, for his own reasons, did not want a vacuum and insisted that the swearing-in of the new Chief Minister should be done on the same day. The party's pleas to conduct the ceremony the following day were not entertained, with the result that the new Chief Minister took oath around 7.30 p.m.

The undaunted Jaya, as if to snipe at her rivals, chose a greenhorn and a first-time legislator, O. Pannerselvam, as her proxy Chief Minister. He was so awed by her that he would not even sit in the same chair in the secretariat, as he revered the seat. He also would not allow his official car to be parked in the portico of Fort St George. He made public statements that he was only temporary and was keeping the seat warm for 'Madam'. Jaya installed Pannerselvam to the disappointment of some senior party leaders, like Deputy Speaker of Lok Sabha Thambi Durai and state Finance Minister, C. Ponnaiyan. Even Pannerselvam was taken aback by the announcement. Those who saw her functioning after the verdict complimented her on the way she handled the crisis. She came out best when fighting her political opponents.

The new Chief Minister began his term only after prostrating himself at Jayalalithaa's feet in full view of all those who attended the swearing-in ceremony. There were no pretensions, though there was some protocol problems as to where should Jaya be seated. Even after stepping down, she was able to create an impression among the public as well as her party members that it was only a temporary measure and she would come back soon. She appealed to the public to be calm and allow the MGR rule to continue.

In the next two-and-a-half months, Jaya did not have much of a problem in running the state through the puppet Chief Minister. Yet, more drama was waiting to unfold. In the game of snakes and ladders, Jaya was again up the ladder. She was on the top when the Tamil Nadu

High Court cleared her in the Tamil Nadu Small Industries Corporation (TANSI) Land case and the Pleasant Stay Hotel case on 4 December 2001. It pertained to allegations that Jaya Publications and Sasi Enterprises, in which Jaya and Sasikala were partners, had bought properties belonging to TANSI at the Guindy Industrial Estate at less than the market rate. This, it was argued, had resulted in a loss of Rs 3.5 crores and Rs 66 lakhs respectively to the state government. Since these properties were bought when Jaya was the Chief Minister, she was accused under the Prevention of Corruption Act. She and her partners were also charged under the Indian Penal Code. In the Pleasant Stay Hotel case, Jayalalithaa, former Local Administration Minister T.M. Selvaganapathy, and three others were accused of regularising the illegal construction of five additional storeys of the hotel in Kodaikanal. On 2 February 2000, special judge V. Radhakrishnan pronounced a one- year rigorous imprisonment to Jaya, and one - year jail to the others. All of them went on to appeal to the High Court.

After the court cleared her, a beaming Jayalalithaa came out and declared: 'There are no legal hurdles now. All legal hurdles have been crossed.' The same evening, there was a legislature party meeting, which had only two items on the agenda. The first was the resignation of Chief Minister Pannerselvam, and the second was the election of Jaya as the party leader again. Although Jaya was facing other cases, she was happy that she was able to re-enter Fort St George and end the absurdity of ruling through proxy. In a way, she had also exhibited political maturity by not rushing to Raj Bhavan as soon as she heard the verdict. In February 2002, she contested from Andipatti, 500 kilometres south of Chennai, and won with a handsome majority. She took over as Chief Minister on 2 March 2002.

Jayalalithaa ruled until 2006. Learning from the past mistakes of her first term, she was more careful and tried to concentrate on developing the state. She told a journalist: 'Is there any human being who has never committed a mistake? The secret of success lies in realising one's mistake, understanding where one went wrong and taking steps to rectify that mistake. A successful leader is one who is flexible. You should not be rigid.'[74] It was during this term that she introduced her landmark Rainwater Harvesting policy that is now a role model across the country and which solved the water problem faced by the state to a certain extent.

Jayalalithaa developed a reputation for having an iron hand on the administration, especially on law and order. A Wikileaks telegram from the US Consulate in Chennai to Washington notes, 'Her tough–on–crime posture was not limited to the LTTE. In 2004, during her second term as Chief Minister, Tamil Nadu police shot and killed the forest bandit Veerappan. He had defied the authorities for decades, killing more than a hundred people (including policemen and forest rangers) while reigning over vast stretches of the state's forests.'[75] As mentioned earlier, Jaya sent a Special Task Force (STF) to the Satyamangalam forests in October 2004 to hunt down the notorious sandalwood smuggler. The sandalwood bandit, as Veerappan was called, had been roaming scot-free in the forests of Tamil Nadu, Karnataka and Kerala, with the connivance of the forest and police officials who feared him. The operation was successful as Veerappan was finally killed by the Special Task Force on 18 November 2004, ending years of his illegal occupation of the forest areas.

However, she did not escape from controversies. Her political vendetta against Karunanidhi continued in her second term. The whole country watched the shocking crackdown on the octogenarian DMK chief at 2 a.m. on 30 June 2001. People witnessed the crackdown telecast on television, with Karunanidhi shouting, 'They are killing me, they are killing me' as the police were pushing him around. They beat up two DMK Central ministers, Murasoli Maran and T.R. Balu, when they intervened. While Karunanidhi was remanded to judicial custody, the two ministers were arrested for blocking the police. When Prime Minister Vajpayee wanted to come to the rescue of the DMK leaders, Jaya, as was her habit, refused to take his phone call. On the contrary, she demanded that the Prime Minister should dismiss the two ministers.

Vajpayee hit back by recalling the Governor, Fatima Beevi. Getting the message loud and clear, Jaya climbed down and released Karunanidhi on what she called humanitarian grounds because of his age. She did not spare her one time ally, Vaiko, the chief of Marumalarchi Dravida Munnetra Kazhagam, either, and put him under a Draconian law, the Prevention of Terrorism Act 2002 (POTA), and kept him in jail for nineteen months.

Kanchi Shankaracharya Jayendra Saraswathi, who has thousands of followers, was charged by the Tamil Nadu government of being a conspirator in the murder of a temple manager Sankararaman in Kanchipuram, on 28 November 2004. As it was not a prima facie case of murder, but simply an accusation that he had conspired to commit a murder, his arrest was seen as premature. There were reports that they wanted to keep him in custody without extending even basic facilities offered to a political prisoner. Jayalalithaa remained as inscrutable as ever, even though the Kanchi pontiff and the Chief Minister were allies in their stand against religious conversions in Meenakshipuram. 'We have established the rule of law,' she justified. 'We have also established that every one is equal before the law,' she told the Assembly. This resulted in bad publicity for Jayalalithaa from his devotees. On 10 January 2005, the Supreme Court granted bail to the god man and the case was later transferred to the neighbouring union territory of Puducherry after the Mutt seers took to a legal recourse, approaching the Supreme Court seeking transfer of the case to any other state. The Kanchi seer was freed later.

Jayalalaihtaa's decision to bring the Anti-conversion Bill in 2002, to check religious conversions, was also her undoing, as it did not work in her favour. There is a history to the bill. Soon after the Mandaikadu Hindu-Christian riots in 1982, the then MGR government appointed the Justice Venugopal Commission to go into the incident. In March 1982, there was a major clash between two communities at Mandaikadu, a coastal village in Kanyakumari district. Six fishermen died due to police firing and forty persons were injured, including twenty-five policemen, during a communal clash between the Christian fishermen and Hindus at the time of Mandaikadu temple festival. Though Justice Venugopal was said to be a Dravidian movement sympathiser, he was shocked by the extent of hate literature and missionary propaganda in the district. In 1986, the MGR government had agreed to the Commission's recommendation that an anti-conversion law similar to the one existing in Odisha, Madhya Pradesh, Tripura and Arunachal Pradesh be enacted in Tamil Nadu. 'So, in a way, the Jayalalithaa government only fulfilled a long-made commitment of her mentor's. But she had underestimated the power of the Church and the evangelical organizations and overestimated the strength of the political Hindu forces in Tamil Nadu.'[76] Jayalaihtaa had also introduced a ban on the sacrifice of animals in temples. So the

DMK-led Opposition launched a virulent campaign linking these laws accusing her of being Brahminical and anti minority. Nearer the 2004 Parliamentary elections, the DMK left the NDA and the AIADMK aligned with the BJP.

Although she got the Act repealed later, when she found it counter-productive, the post-poll analysis showed that a large number of Muslims voted for the DMK alliance because they were angry at the way Jaya brought in the anti-conversion law and also apprehensive about the misuse of it. The 2004 disastrous results for her party made her think about it and she got them reversed but the religious leaders continued to be annoyed.

An electorally humiliated Jayalalithaa announced on 21 May 2005: 'Following representations from minorities, I had announced on May 13, 2004, that the law would be repealed and an ordinance was promulgated on May 18 the same year.'[77]

Jaya was also tough with the bureaucrats. It was a well-known fact that she kept them on their toes, and they were made to implement her orders. She regularly punished the errant officers who displeased her by suspending or transferring them to unpleasant assignments and locations. A Wikileaks telegram from Chennai to Washington notes that 'Jayalalithaa was hard on the state's bureaucrats. She regularly punished civil servants. For example, she summarily suspended her Home Secretary for supporting bail for an accused in a terrorist bombing case. The Home Secretary had supported the bail plea on humanitarian grounds, as the accused was physically ill. In 2003 Jayalalithaa dismissed 17,000 striking government employees: a court reinstated them shortly thereafter. But the decision came back to haunt Jayalalithaa as the ire of the fired employees and their families is believed to have played a significant role in the electoral drubbing the AIADMK took in 2004.'[78]

After she became the Chief Minister for the first time, in 1991, Jayalalithaa slowly stripped the powers of the Chief Secretary, the top civil servant in the state, and concentrated them on her Chief Minister's office, which became all powerful, just as Indira Gandhi made her Prime Minister's office powerful. When she got rid of the Chief Secretary P. Shankar, in 2001, an officer with high integrity, it was Prime Minister Vajpayee who came to his rescue and accommodated him in the Planning Commission. She also made the officers bend every rule to suit her convenience. It was her way of concentrating power in her hands. *The Times of India* notes, 'Her trusted lieutenants could do anything as long as they kept her in the loop. But if they lost her trust, she would not hesitate to sack them. The suspensions of former Chief Secretary K. Gnanadesikan (2016) and former DGP A. Ravindranath (2001) are examples. It's not just within the state that she had admirers. A senior police officer recalls a group of officials from another state commenting, after a meeting with Jayalalithaa: "You perhaps have the best chief minister in the country." They were bowled over by her understanding of issues, clarity of thought and succinct speech.'[79]

The National Democratic Alliance, while working on its 'India Shining' campaign, lost to the United Progressive Alliance (UPA). Congress President Sonia Gandhi had built up this coalition by mobilising anti-BJP parties in 2004 just before the Parliamentary elections. By this time, Karunanidhi had teamed up with the Congress-led UPA. In Tamil Nadu, the DMK, Congress, MDMK and PMK combined together and contested the elections. The DMK was on the upswing again, and won sixteen seats, while the Congress won ten; the PMK won five, and the MDMK got four seats; the CPI and Communist Party of India (Marxist) (CPI-M) got two seats each. The AIADMK and the BJP got no seats. The DMK became a partner in the UPA government at the Centre, and bagged important ministries. Jaya could see the voters' anger against her rule.

Jayalalithaa learnt her lessons and tried to change her tactics and bring populist measures to woo the gullible voters and win the 2006 Assembly polls. By this time, her dominance over her party became absolute and she insisted on personally clearing even the smallest matters. She changed her advisers frequently, never allowing them to become powerful enough or take advantage of their access to her.

However, as expected, Jaya lost the 2006 Assembly elections and the DMK, led by Karunanidhi, rode to power. Karunanidhi outdid Jayalalithaa in announcing freebees, including colour TVs, cheap rice and gas connections, which got him votes from the poor, and the rural folks. Although, taking a cue from him, Jaya, too, competed with him and announced more freebees, but it did not help.

Karunanidhi became the Chief Minister of Tamil Nadu for the fifth time, forming a minority government in 2006. The DMK alliance got 45 per cent of vote share (ninety-six seats), while the AIADMK alliance got 40 per cent vote share (sixty-one seats); with support from allies like the Congress, the Karunanidhi-led party managed to sail through. The DMK remained a 'minority government' throughout its five-year tenure (2006-11) as Karunanidhi did not want to share power with the alliance partners despite the fact that the Congress had won thirty-four out of the forty-eight seats it contested, showing a bigger strike rate.

There were at least four reasons for the DMK's victory. The first was the usual anti-incumbency factor which came into play; people wanted a change as they were vexed by the autocratic and corrupt rule of Jaya and the several controversies involving her. Even otherwise, Tamil Nadu had been alternating between the DMK and the AIADMK, and it was now the turn of the DMK, in 2006.

The second reason was the viable and strong coalition which Karunanidhi had built up with the Congress and some other smaller parties. It was the arithmetic which began to matter in coalition politics. The third reason was the freebees that the DMK announced—the colour televisions and mixer-grinders. The fourth reason was the entry of a new player—Captain Vijayakant, the film actor-turned–politician—in electoral politics. He earned the nickname 'Captain' after the stupendous success of his film *Captain Prabhakaran* in 1990. Captain Vijayakant succeeded to a certain extent by exploiting the anger of the people against the government, and struck a chord with the common man. His popularity as well as novelty contributed to his party Desiya Murpokku Dravida Kazhagam (DMDK) getting about 10 per cent of the votes, which mainly cut into the AIADMK votes in 2006. In 2011, Vijayakanth won his Assembly seat with a huge margin of over 30,000 votes. He also went in for an alliance with the AIADMK and won twenty-nine MLAs in 2011. But he ran into rough weather when eight of his MLAs joined the ruling AIADMK before 2014. He drew a blank in the 2014 polls. In the run up to the 2016 elections, the Captain projected himself as the chief ministerial candidate. His party's downslide by this time was complete, and the party won no seats.

The other reason for the AIADMK loss was that Jayalalithaa was openly declaring that she was going to have a post–poll alliance with the BJP. This put off some anti–BJP voters who were disenchanted with the NDA rule.

So after she was dumped by the Tamil Nadu electorate, Jaya was languishing politically. She had lost two consecutive—2004 Lok Sabha and 2006 Assembly—polls, but that did not dampen the fighting spirit of the AIADMK supremo. She was getting ready to face the 2009 Lok Sabha polls. This time, she thought things would work in her favour because of the people's fatigue with the DMK which was facing several problems, including family feuds, indiscipline and factionalism. Karunanidhi, who has been leading the party from 1969, after the death of its founder C.N. Annadurai, had made the party subservient to his family. His younger son M.K. Stalin was the deputy Chief Minister, while elder son M.K. Azhagiri was a Central cabinet minister in the UPA regime. His daughter Kanimozhi was the chief of the DMK women's wing, while Karunanidhi's grand-nephew, Dayanidhi Maran, was the Telecom Minister at the Centre. Stalin and Azhagiri were fighting for Karunanidhi's legacy within the party while Kanimozhi, who also became an MP, was ambitious. His grand-nephew was another family member vying for influence. This in-fighting was one of the reasons for Jaya's hopes. The DMK patriarch continued to be the peacemaker between his sons and daughter Kanimozhi. He resolved this by dumping Azhagiri, while the other two patched up.

The DMK ousted its partner, Pattali Makkal Katchi (PMK), at the state level, although Karunanidhi did not object to the PMK ministers continuing in the Manmohan Singh government. Secondly, the Indo-US nuclear deal was becoming controversial and the Left parties, which were opposed to the deal, did not like the DMK supporting the deal. The CPI and the CPI-M, after withdrawing support to the Manmohan Singh government in 2008 on the Indo-Nuclear deal with the US felt that aligning with the AIADMK at the national level might be better and, therefore, joined the AIADMK coalition during the 2009 Lok Sabha polls in Tamil Nadu.

However, despite the 2G spectrum allocation scam affecting Karunanidhi's family, besides other corruption charges faced by him, the UPA came back to power with more number of seats and Manmohan Singh became the Prime Minister of India for a second time.

The 2G spectrum allocation was a major scam detected by the Comptroller and Auditor General Vinod Rai. Rai had detected irregularities in the spectrum project that cost the Union Government a notional loss of Rs 1.76 lakh crores. It was alleged that licenses were issued to private telecom players at throw away prices. The Telecom Minister A. Raja belonged to the DMK. Rai's report was placed in Parliament on 16 November 2010.

Moreover, the Sri Lankan government wiping out the LTTE and the genocide of the innocent civilians during the Eelam war 4 was also a factor in the 2009 polls, with Karunanidhi being accused of not helping the Tamils. Surprisingly, the UPA contingent from Tamil Nadu won twenty-seven of the thirty-nine seats, with DMK getting eighteen seats, the Congress eight, and Vidudalai Chiruttai Katchi (VCK) one seat. Even the UPA did not expect such a bonanza. The AIADMK coalition, on the other hand, won only twelve seats of which the AIADMK got nine, CPI, CPI-M and MDMK got one each. However, the AIADMK got 39.1 per cent of the vote share whereas the DMK got 44.9 per cent. The tally from zero in 2004 to nine in 2009 enthused Jaya. The DMDK retained its ten per cent vote share with no seats. The AIADMK allies MDMK and PMK lost out with zero seats. Jaya, who was planning to visit Delhi if she had won to become a national player, remained indoors without talking to anyone while the DMK-Congress ties got cemented further after the election results.

Jayalalithaa did not give up even after the poor election results in the 2009 Lok Sabha polls and was getting ready to face the 2011 Assembly polls even after consecutively losing in 2004, 2006 and 2009. She changed her strategy and hit the roads for mass contact programme. She toured the length and breadth of the state preparing for the polls and addressing the voters directly in simple language. She activated her cadres and did everything to boost their morale despite not being in power both at the Centre or in the state.

Jaya was looking for issues to attack the Karunanidhi government and she fortunately got them on a platter. Karunanidhi's wife Dayalu Ammal, grand-nephew Dayanidhi Maran, and daughter Kanimozhi were alleged to have been involved in the 2G telecom scam, facing court cases. Kanimozhi had been named as a co-accused and had been charge-sheeted by the CBI for allegedly accepting Rs 214 crores as bribe. The DMK MP and Dalit leader A. Raja had been in Tihar jail in New Delhi since February 2011, for allegedly planning and executing the 2G scam when he was Telecom Minister, in 2008. Kanimozhi was jailed on 20 May 2011. This developed strains in the Congress–DMK relationship, although Karunanidhi did not pull out his party's support to the Manmohan Singh government. That came much later, on the Sri Lankan Tamil issue, in 2013.

In this adverse atmosphere for the DMK came the 2011 Assembly polls. Jaya used it to her full advantage and the anti-incumbency factor also worked in her favour with the result the AIADMK combination came back to power. It won a massive majority winning an impressive 203 of the 234 seats. She was able to pull this off as she had got her arithmetic right and had aligned with the CPI, the CPI-M, the DMDK and other smaller parties. The alliance got 51.9 per cent vote share while the AIADMK alone got 38.4 per cent, winning 150 seats on its own. The DMK won twenty-three seats and a vote share of 22.4 per cent. The BJP got zero seats with 2.2 per cent vote share.

Moreover as former National Security Adviser M.K. Narayanan notes: 'She scrupulously avoided tampering with the politics of caste, realising the fundamental importance of the caste arithmetic in Tamil Nadu politics. In particular, she took care not to disturb existing equations involving major caste groups, understanding that she was an "outlier" as far as dominant castes in the politics of Tamil Nadu were concerned. While maintaining the supremacy of the caste structure, she essentially confined herself to providing a new twist and imparting a new meaning to welfare economics.'[80]

Jaya triumphantly entered the government secretariat again as Chief Minister on 16 May 2011, followed by a historical triumph in 2016. The change in Jaya was visible when she allowed AIADMK supporters to enter her bungalow gates in Poes Garden while the counting was going on and those who knew her said she was mellowed in her third term.

The first thing she did was to relocate the new state-of-the-art Rs 425 crore Tamil Nadu Assembly complex in Chennai, built on an area of over 80,000 square meters, a pet project of her predecessor, Karunanidhi, back to Fort St George. Built with the expertise of a German architectural firm and incorporating elements of the Dravidian style, the new Assembly complex came up where the heritage Admiralty House and CB-CID office (home to the Governor during British rule) once stood, on the Omandurar government estate. As the then Leader of Opposition, Jayalalithaa opposed the construction of the complex. By the time the building was completed, Karunanidhi was on his way out. Jayalalithaa, on 19 August 2011, announced in the Assembly that the new complex would be converted into a hospital, dashing the dreams of Karunanidhi. 'Jayalalithaa, who had criticised the project as a "wasteful expenditure" and described the structure as a "circus tent", for lack of aesthetic appeal, had announced a probe into the alleged irregularities in the construction. The Chief Minister continued to function from Fort St George, which was the seat of power before the new complex came up, asserting that her move was not prompted by political consideration but determined by administrative reasons.[81]

Her big challenge was the revamping of the state's economy. Tamil Nadu had a debt of over one lakh crore rupees. As *India Today* notes: "Fiscal deficit is large at over Rs 13,507 crore (financial year 2011-12), state's GDP growth has slowed and it is deep in debt. The state's borrowing is set to exceed Rs 1 lakh crore this fiscal. Per capita debt is estimated at around Rs 14,700."[82] Knowing the gravity of the situation, Jaya announced in her first interaction with the press that the DMK had ruined Tamil Nadu's economy and her first priority would be to set it right. Also, she had announced many freebees during her campaign which also needed to be delivered. The other priority was to restore law and order. In her third term as Chief Minister, she also had to face challenges such as the prolonged anti-nuclear agitation in the south, holding up work on the commissioning of the Kudankulam power project with two 1,000 MW reactors, the emotive issue of treatment of Tamils in Sri Lanka, and the inter-state water disputes with Kerala and Karnataka.

After winning a third term, Jaya was looking for a raised profile. She consolidated herself further, hoping to play a bigger role in national politics. She believed all this while that there would be another coalition government in the 2014 Lok Sabha polls in which she would have a major stake. Even before that, she got some international publicity when, in 2011, the United States Secretary of state, Hillary Clinton, visited Chennai and called on the Chief Minister on 20 July. It was a significant high profile visit. It flagged a new dynamism in India's foreign policy, which was increasing the role of provinces. In an unusual manner, Clinton discussed the bilateral strategy on the Sri Lankan Tamil issue with Jaya. Taking the opportunity, Jayalalithaa requested Hillary to make investments in Tamil Nadu in the automobile sector, solar energy and road infrastructure development. 'More broadly, the Secretary of state and Chief Minister Jayalalithaa talked about how there needs to be greater progress towards reconciliation and that really, the government should redouble its efforts to reach an agreement in their dialogue with the Tamil National Alliance on all of the key issues of concern to Tamils inside Sri Lanka,' Robert Blake, the US assistant Secretary of state, who accompanied Clinton, said.[83]

Jaya brought the Sri Lankan issue to the fore during her meeting with Hillary. The *Economist* magazine put it succinctly: 'How then should leading Tamil politicians, such as the Chief Minister, who are trying to position themselves to be influential in 2014 (Lok Sabha elections) go about building support among their voters in the coming months? One natural answer is to bash Sri Lankan rulers and speak up for Tamils across the water, make a loud fuss when votes are expected on war crimes in the United Nations, criticise Delhi's ruling class as supine in the face of Sinhalese nationalists and keep alive tensions between the two countries. Indian Tamils care strongly about the issue, so there is an opportunity for both to attack the ruling Congress Party and just possibly influence foreign policy. For Miss Jayalalithaa the closer the national elections loomed in India, the greater the reason to inveigh against the wicked Sinhalese in Colombo. If this analysis is right, India's internal politics will discourage warm ties with Sri Lanka until at least 2014 and probably beyond.'[84] So it was not surprising that Jaya got many resolutions passed in the Tamil Nadu Assembly in favour of Sri Lankan Tamils, and also led the agitation against the Sri Lankan government putting pressure on the Manmohan Singh government. The DMK withdrew from the UPA government in 2013 on the Tamil issue.

Jayalalithaa also played pressure politics at the national level. She became part of the United National Progressive Alliance (UNPA), a group of eight parties, which were neither part of the UPA or the NDA, nor the Left wing. Jayalalithaa took lead in mobilising support for Kalam. This group had approached President A.P.J. Kalam to contest presidential elections in 2007 and Samajwadi Party leader Rashid Masood was their vice presidential candidate. Kalam refused to contest. Ultimately, the UPA candidate Pratibha Patil won the Presidency. Though the Samajwadi Party (SP) also supported Kalam, it also later supported the UPA when it went for a trust vote.

She took lead in the 2012 presidential elections by supporting former Speaker Purno Agitok Sangma against the UPA nominee Pranab Mukherji. She joined hands with her Odisha counterpart Naveen Patnaik in supporting Sangma, knowing very well that Mukherji enjoyed wide popular support. Sangma's own party, the Nationalist Congress Party (NCP), distanced itself from supporting his candidature. Justifying her stand on the candidature of Sangma, she said, 'During the past 60 years of the Republic of India, while eminent personalities belonging to various communities and diverse walks of life have graced the office of the Rashtrapathi, no one belonging to a tribal community has had the opportunity so far.'[85] She teamed up with her Odisha counterpart Naveen Patnaik, who also simultaneously supported Sangma's candidature in Bhubaneswar. Ironically, even Sangma's Nationalist Congress Party did not support him.

'The AIADMK chief got in touch with a number of national leaders to seek support for Mr Sangma. She spoke on the phone to senior BJP leader L.K. Advani; Communist Party of India (Marxist) general secretary Prakash Karat; senior CPI leader A.B. Bardhan; Telugu Desam Party president Chandrababu Naidu; Samajwadi Party chief and former Uttar Pradesh Chief Minister Mulayam Singh and Shiromani Akali Dal leader and Punjab Chief Minister Parkash Singh Badal.'[86]

There was little doubt that the veteran leader Pranab Mukherji would sail through; the results of the presidential poll between Mukherjee and Sangma were no surprise. Jaya also backed dissident BJP leader Jaswant Singh for the post of Vice President and he lost to the UPA candidate Hamid Ansari.

She teamed up with non-Congress Chief Ministers like Narendra Modi, Naveen Patnaik and others when the Manmohan Singh government wanted to create a National Counter Terrorism Centre (NCTC), resulting in the Union government backing out. She invited Narendra Modi for her swearing-in ceremony in May 2011, when she won a third term, and returned the favour when Modi won his third term in 2012.

She discovered that the best way to remain in power would be through social welfare schemes; hence, she designed several innovative ones. Whatever discontent there was amongst the masses, it was offset by these schemes, which were well received. She portrayed herself as the champion of poor by introducing schemes like cheap food, cheap medicines, even mineral water and cement. She won a substantial percentage of women's votes, both in 2011 and 2016. She did so by appealing to the women voters both in an overt as well as subtle way: Twenty kilos of rice for each Below Poverty Line (BPL) family, numbering about

1.58 crores, mixer-grinders, free fans, Amma canteens selling curd rice, and snacks like idli and vada at affordable prices, and a *taali* (*mangalsutra*) for brides; even Amma cement, Amma mineral water, and Amma pharmacies selling cheap medicines, to name a few. All these benefitted the common man, and they were appreciated. Jaya also exploited the caste and gender considerations. She smartly countered the DMK's support base—the Other Backward Classes (OBCs)—by building a coalition of higher castes: The Dalits, and the core group of the OBCs, Thevars, to which her constant companion Sasikala belongs. She wooed women and won their confidence in 2011, and even later in the 2014 Lok Sabha and 2016 Assembly elections.

To boost the economy of the state, she launched the Vision 2023 Programmes, where she visualised an investment of $ 250 billion to flow in. Launching the industrial plan, Jayalalithaa outlined her ambitious vision saying: 'To achieve the goals relating to manufacturing two sets of Memorandum of Understandings numbering 17 in all were signed in my presence in 2012, committing an investment of Rs 26,625 crores. Today (February 22, 2014) 16 more MOUs are being signed for industries with a total investment of Rs 5081 crores offering employment to 16, 282 persons. With this the total investment envisaged in the 33 MOUs signed so far by my government in its present tenure is Rs 31,706 crore with an employment potential for over 1,62,667 persons. I have often said that the investment is an act of faith based on rational expectations. It is a vote of confidence.'[87]

'I feel it is essential to tell the 5,62,06,547 voters covered in 64,094 polling stations on behalf of the AIADMK that Tamil Nadu is marching on a growth path never seen before due to efforts aimed at people's development,' she said in a party release in Chennai before the poll campaign in 2016, aware of the need to propagate her achievements. The government also claimed to have recruited over 70,000 teachers and provided liberal funds for infrastructural projects. Young children studying in government schools were given free notebooks, textbooks including atlases, uniforms, geometry boxes, and chappals. They were also given colour pencils, crayons, chessboards and school bags, all free of cost. Older students studying in government and aided schools and colleges received free laptops. Free bicycles were distributed to students of Class XII in government and aided schools.

She reaped the fruits in the 2014 polls when a massive swing of 21.3 per cent in vote share propelled the AIADMK to a resounding victory, with Jayalalithaa stunning everyone by winning thirty-seven of the thirty-nine seats in Tamil Nadu and emerging as the third largest party in the Lok Sabha. Women came out in large numbers and supported her, forming her core constituency. If she was able to come back to power in the 2016 Assembly elections, it was because women stood by her. They were impressed by the welfare schemes, including Pongal gift packs, an assistance of Rs 18,000 to each pregnant woman under the Dr Muthulakshmi Reddy maternity benefit scheme, a marriage assistance scheme of Rs 50,000 to women who are graduates or diploma holders, distribution of eight grams of gold free of cost for making mangalsutra (a pendant worn at the time of marriage), the Chief Minister's girl child protection scheme, six months of maternity leave to women who are employed with the government, and distribution of baby care kits.

The crestfallen DMK not only had a 1.6 per cent drop in vote share in the 2014 election from 25 per cent in 2009, but also suffered a major jolt as it did not win a single seat. In 2009, the DMK had won eighteen seats scoring 25 per cent of the total votes polled. In 2014, the Congress got just 4.3 per cent vote share as opposed to the 20 per cent earlier, and no seats. The AIADMK had thirteen MPs in the Rajya Sabha, which gives the party a national clout, as the AIADMK commands the fourth position in the Upper House of the Parliament. By controlling forty-eight MPs in both houses of Parliament, Jayalalithaa had become almost indispensable, particularly when the BJP was in a minority in the Upper House. The Modi government needed the AIADMK support on important legislations like the Goods and Services Tax, Land Acquisition and other reform measures which were stuck in the Parliament.

Jayalalithaa had steered clear of forging any alliance with either of the two national parties—the BJP or the Congress in 2014. Things were going well for her until her fourth year in office. It was speculated that she would join hands with the BJP in the 2014 Lok Sabha polls as she had good equations with the BJP's prime ministerial candidate, Narendra Modi. But to everyone's surprise, she refused to do so despite overtures from the BJP. It was not a whimsical decision, but based on pure arithmetic. In 1991, the Congress-AIADMK coalition won thirty-nine seats but the AIADMK won only eleven seats. In the 2004 coalition with the BJP, the AIADMK lost rural votes and the BJP could hardly transfer any votes to the AIADMK, yet it won twenty-eight seats. Her decision to go alone all the way paid her rich dividends as the AIADMK won thirty-seven of the thirty-nine seats, practically reducing the other parties to zero.

Jaya suffered a legal and political setback once again on 17 September 2014 when the trial court convicted and sentenced her to four years jail in an eighteen-year-old corruption case. The judgment unseated her from the

Chief Minister's chair and disqualified her immediately as an MLA. The case dates back to 1996 when the BJP leader Dr Subramanian Swamy (he was then with the Janata Party) registered a complaint against Jayalalithaa that the latter's financial assets soared from Rs 2.6 crores to Rs 66.65 crores during her first term as Chief Minister of Tamil Nadu, between 1991–1996. The special judge, John Michael D'Cunha, also slapped a fine of Rs 100 crores, apart from the jail term. The problem of disqualification arose because unless the conviction was stayed or overturned by a superior court, she could not become the Chief Minister in future.

When the Karnataka designated trial court convicted her on 27 September 2014, many thought that this would be the end of Jayalalithaa's political career. The trial court sentenced her and three other co-accused, including Sasikala, to four years in jail in the Rs 66.54 crores Disproportionate Assets case filed in 1996. It also slapped a hefty penalty of Rs 100 crores on Jayalalithaa. Many of her supporters thought that this was too high a punishment.

Undaunted, Jaya found a way to overcome this situation, too. She decided, on her remote control strategy once again, to install a puppet Chief Minister who would hold the seat warm for her until she was cleared. She rewarded O. Pannerselvam for the loyalty he had displayed earlier, and once again made him the Chief Minister, on 29 September 2014. Overwhelmed by emotions, and with tears in his eyes, Pannerselvam took oath along with thirty other ministers who were equally grim at the swearing-in ceremony. In a show of loyalty, he took out a small photograph of Jayalalithaa and placed it on the lectern while repeating the oath of office and secrecy. He is reported to have kept Jaya's slippers by his side, following the simile from the epic Ramayana, when prince Bharat kept the sandals of his elder brother Ram by his side during his absence. Pannerselvam functioned from his existing Finance Minister's office and did not use the Chief Minister's chamber when he became Chief Minister for the second time. He was once reported to have said that his initial was not the alphabet 'O' but 'zero', because that was all he was in comparison to his leader. Even when he was sworn in for the third time after the death of Jayalalithaa, a grim-faced Pannerselvam, with the photograph of his departed leader in his shirt pocket in a transparent manner, took oath in a solemn ceremony. During the initial weeks of Jaya's hospitalisation in 2016, he kept her portrait behind him when he held meetings. On 18 October 2016, *The Mint* newspaper reported that Pannerselvam chaired a meeting of the state Cabinet with a picture of Jayalalithaa on his desk, and the government released photographs of the meeting.

As earlier, Jaya ruled Tamil Nadu by remote control until she returned in 2015, when the Karnataka High Court acquitted her of the Disproportionate Assets case on May 11. However, the administration suffered because Pannerselvam was not taking any decisions. Two major initiatives—the inauguration of the Chennai Metro and a Global Investors' Meet—were delayed because of Jaya's absence from the office.

But her cadres did not lose faith in her. True to their expectations, a year later, she returned as Chief Minister. Jayalalithaa got a major relief when the Supreme Court granted her conditional bail and suspended the sentence of four years simple imprisonment given by the trial court in Bengaluru. She was released on October 18, after spending twenty-one days in the Bengaluru central jail. This was the second span of imprisonment. Earlier, the DMK government in Tamil Nadu had her arrested in the television scam case in December 1996, also during her (first) term as Chief

Minister, from 1991-96. Arrested on 7 December 1996, she had spent twenty-seven days in Chennai's central jail before being released on bail in January 1997. But then, she had been an under trial prisoner. Now, she was a convicted prisoner.

Jayalalithaa got relief when the Karnataka High Court acquitted her on 11 May 2015, paving way for her retrun to become the Chief Minister again. Justice Kumaraswamy, from the Karnataka High Court, who acquitted her and her associates in the case, refused to take into account the value of apparel and slippers seized from Jayalalithaa's home, terming it 'insignificant'. The High Court said the prosecution had 'failed to appreciate the evidence in proper perspective'. It said the immovable properties in the names of Jayalalithaa and the co-accused had been acquired by borrowing huge loans from nationalised banks but the prosecution had wrongly failed to include the loans in the income figures. Although the FIR accused Jayalalithaa of benami transactions of large agricultural tracts and a tea estate, the court found no evidence of it. The High Court said the burden of proof lay on the prosecution, which had failed to prove the charges. 'Accused No. 1 (Jayalalithaa) is a cine actress. She has filed returns since she was a minor,' the court said. It noted that Jayalalithaa's mother had purchased the Poes Garden residence and that the AIADMK leader had bought only the adjacent property, for Rs 8 lakh. 'When the principal accused has been acquitted, the other accused who have played a lesser role are also entitled for acquittal,' the court ruled.[88]

The judgment was undoubtedly a resounding political victory for Jayalalithaa as she claimed that in a way it removed the taint of corruption that had damaged her political reputation. The acquittal enabled her to reassume public office, that too at a time the 2016 Assembly polls were just months away. She came home with thousands of cadres cheering her all the way. It was indeed unusual for any politician in the country to regain eligibility to hold the post after being legally unseated twice as Chief Minister. On both occasions, this was possible because a High Court intervened to reverse the conviction recorded by trial courts. Even legally, the Disproportionate Assets case was the strongest among the cases she faced. So Jaya returned to Fort St George with complete political and moral authority. The Karnataka government moved the Supreme Court against the acquittal of Jayalalithaa and Sasikala, and the other accused on 23 June 2015. On 7 June 2016, the apex court reserved its verdict on the appeal. Jaya died on 5 December 2016. The Supreme Court set aside on 14 February 2017 Sasikala's—by now she had become the AIADMK general secretary—Disproportionate Assets case and restored 'in full' the trial court's conviction of September 2014. Jaya's name was removed because she was dead but the penalty of Rs 100 crores would be realised from her assets.

After her acquittal by the Karnataka High Court, Jayalalithaa was sworn in as Chief Minister for the fifth time, on 23 May 2015, nearly nine months after she stepped down. There was a sigh of relief from the pubic as they were fed up with the policy paralysis during the proxy rule by Pannerselvam. True to their expectations, on the first day itself, Jaya set the state machinery rolling by signing several welfare schemes. She got down to business by launching 201 Amma canteens which sold food at reasonable prices, and sixteen Amma pharmacies which provided cheap medicine. She also signed a Rs 1,800 crore development project along with Rs 100 crore employment training schemes for women, apart from supply of cheaper pulses. Jaya began to prepare for the 2016 elections with a determination to come back. She sought votes on her performance and the numerous welfare schemes.

With a weakened DMK and other opposition parties, she would have sailed through easily in the 2016 elections. However, there was a setback as Tamil Nadu, particularly Chennai, faced the rain fury in December 2015 and suffered huge damages, with thousands of people rendered homeless and the city inundated. It was said to be a rain fury of unprecedented nature in the last 100 years. Since the administration was taken unawares, there was some slackness initially but soon Jayalalithaa cracked the whip and the relief and rehabilitation measures were taken up on a war footing. She promptly sought financial relief from the Centre for about Rs 2,000 crores, but Prime Minister Modi released Rs 940 crores as an immediate help. The BJP was also aiming to make some improvement on its chances in the 2016 polls and so the Prime Minister not only visited Chennai immediately but also provided the much needed financial package.

When the 2016 Assembly polls came, Jayalalithaa thought that the sympathy wave after her court victory on the Disproportionate Assets case would help her because many thought that a Rs 100 crore fine was a little too much for a crime of Rs 60 odd crores of illegal assets. Anti-incumbency was heavily weighed against the ruling party in some districts including Kanchipuram. By conventional logic, she should not have won the elections after the rain havoc, but to the surprise of all, she came back with a handsome majority for the second consecutive election in a row, immensely benefitting from a fractured political field. The last Tamil Nadu Chief Minister to be voted back to power for a second consecutive term was the legendary M.G. Ramachandran

The AIADMK had fought the 2016 polls alone, leaving no alliance options for smaller parties. Tamil Nadu had never seen such a close result in the past. Although Jayalihtaa's AIADMK performed well, the DMK's performance was not bad either. After being decimated in the 2011 Assembly and 2014 Lok Sabha polls, the DMK came back with ninety-eight seats along with its allies and also revived the majority of its vote share.

The DMK emerged as a strong opposition. The AIADMK had a strong rural vote and Jayalalithaa's outreach was a big factor. Playing a martyr, she impressed upon the people in her public meetings saying, 'My ascetic life is dedicated for you, my work is for your upliftment and your joy is my goal.' Among the slew of development works she listed in Chennai include metro rail, drinking water schemes, desalination plants, and cleaning up of Cooum river, all of which were worth many hundreds of crores.

How did the AIADMK win the 2016 polls? There was a marked difference in people's perception of promises made by the two major Dravidian parties. They by and large rejected DMK's poll pledges and its offer of freebees. The Chennai floods exposed the government's weaknesses but the DMK could not capitalize on the ruling party's obvious failures. It also could not benefit from the reports of poor health and selective public appearances of Jayalalithaa. The unresolved family rivalries saw Karunanidhi's elder son, M.K. Azhagiri, staying away from this election, which gave the AIADMK an upper hand in his Madurai strongholds. 'This election has upheld true democracy shattering to pieces the campaign of lies of DMK. This election has put a permanent full stop to the family rule,' Jayalalithaa declared in a statement as her party forged ahead in the counting of votes polled in the 2016 Assembly elections. The DMK's alliance with the Congress also proved to be costly. The Congress had to live down its role in the Eelam War 4, which killed thousands of Tamils, with the Congress-led UPA government at the Centre being blamed for standing by as an onlooker.

To Jayalalithaa's advantage, the anti-establishment votes got fragmented across the three main competing opposition groups—the DMK-Congress alliance, the PMK and the six-party People's Welfare Front (PWF). For the first time, the CPI and the CPI-M did not win a single seat. As journalist Nirupama Subramanian writes: 'It has to be Jayalalithaa's good fortune that in the popular public mind, the DMK remains a "2G-corruption" tainted party but corruption charges against her or the AIADMK don't stick as much. In many places, reminders about the on-going Disproportionate Assets case against her were met with a shrug and a counter question: And the DMK is clean? Jayalalithaa's rumoured ill-health also did not matter. For one thing, the immediate comparison was with the wheelchair-bound Karunanidhi. Die-hard AIADMK supporters don't believe anything could be wrong with her health, just as many of them still continue to vote for the AIADMK in the belief that MGR never died.'[89] The DMDK chief Vijayakant not only lost his seat but also his deposit and brought down the vote share of his party to one fourth of the 10 per cent vote share he had obtained earlier. The BJP too saw a marginal increase in its vote share to 2.8 per cent from 2.01 per cent in 2011; it did not gain many seats.

It was not surprising, because since the 1991 Assembly elections, the AIADMK has fallen behind the DMK in vote share only once, in 1996, when the anti-incumbency factor worked against Jayalalithaa. On other occasions, the party has won more votes than the DMK, even when it contested forty-two seats less than the DMK (2001) or when it lost the election (2006). Between 1996 and 2016, there have been eight elections in Tamil Nadu—five Lok Sabha and three Assembly. The DMK secured more votes than the AIADMK in only one election, in 2009. Even then, the difference in vote share was a mere

2.21 percentage points. This was true even when the AIADMK had no major allies.

In her victory speech thanking the people, Jaya said: 'Although ten political parties have contested against the AIADMK, I aligned with the people of Tamil Nadu and believed in god.' Addressing the supporters from the balcony of her Poes Garden residence, she said: 'I am overwhelmed by the resounding victory the people of Tamil Nadu have given us. My party and I are indebted to the people of Tamil Nadu for giving this historic victory,' as hundreds of supporters swarmed outside her house. Though she was still one term short of her bête noire and DMK chief Karunanidhi's five terms, Jayalalithaa had outstripped that of her mentor MGR, who led his party to three consecutive terms and remained Chief Minister from 1977 to 1987. It was also the first time since MGR's time that a sitting Chief Minister won the polls for a second consecutive term.

While Jayalalithaa spoke of the Sri Lankan Tamils during her campaign before the 2011 Lok Sabha polls, most Tamil Nadu parties competed with each other in raising the Sri Lankan Tamil issue. Jayalalithaa's response to the Northern Province (of Sri Lanka) Chief Minister Wigneswaran's greetings on her victory indicated how she would take up the Sri Lankan Tamil issue further. In a letter written to him, Jayalalithaa said: 'In the last five years as the chief minister of Tamil Nadu, I have taken all possible efforts within my power to protect the welfare of the Sri Lankan Tamils and ensure justice due to them. I will continue to take efforts to ensure justice due to the Sri Lankan Tamils of the Northern Province of Sri Lanka, through the government of India.'[90] She reciprocated Wigneswaran's interest in meeting her suggesting, 'We shall meet on a day convenient to both of us.'

As former National Security Adviser M.K. Narayanan observed in an article after Jayalalithaa's demise, 'She understood where to be flexible and where to be rigid. While scrupulously avoiding tampering with the politics of caste, she imparted a new meaning to welfare economics. None of this can, however, erase the fact that she was paranoid when it came to criticism of her actions or policies. She maintained a tight control over the administrative and security apparatus and was unforgiving of anyone who deviated even the slightest from her set prescriptions. She kept her eye on the ball at all times, which possibly was the secret of her success. As far as the people of Tamil Nadu were concerned, the balance sheet of her years in office was positive—a sentiment that led to her truly epic victory in the 2016 Assembly elections.'[91]

Within hours of taking over in her fourth term, on 23 May 2016, Jaya put into practice many things promised in her party manifesto. They included orders for all students in government-run schools to get free breakfast, all newly-married women to get eight grams of gold to make traditional jewellery (earlier the limit was four grams), 500 government-run liquor shops to shut down and store timings reduced by two hours, crop loans of farmers to be waived off, and 100 units of free power for domestic electricity consumers. Banning liquor in the state was the main pre-poll promise that was made during her campaign. While her opponents had promised a direct ban, she had promised a phased ban in which liquor would be completely phased out from the state within a couple of years.

Jayalalithaa began the term well, receiving greetings from Prime Minister Narendra Modi. In fact, when she was acquitted in her Disproportionate Assets case Modi called her up and congratulated her, signalling their friendship which had grown over the years when the two had been

Chief Ministers. In June 2016, she made a visit to New Delhi—her first after her resounding victory—and handed over a 13-point memorandum to the Prime Minister. Among her demands were the formation of a Cauvery Management Board and a Cauvery Water Regulation Committee, restoration of water level at Mullaperiyar to 152 feet, and the interlinking of rivers. The Sri Lankan Tamils issue, lifting of the ban on the conduct of Jallikattu, and declaring Tamil as an official language were also among the demands made by the Chief Minister. Jayalalithaa, in her memorandum, urged the Centre to consider dual citizenship for the Sri Lankan Tamils residing in Tamil Nadu as refugees. Before she could get the Centre's help in all these measures, she lost her life.

TOWARDS THE END...

Jayalalithaa got admitted to the Apollo Hospital on 22 September 2016, complaining of chest congestion and breathing problems; she was also highly diabetic. Since then, until December 5, when she passed away, her party maintained that she was well and would come back home. The goodwill for her was evident when several leaders including Prime Minister Modi and other national leaders wished her well and some even visited the hospital only to come back without seeing her during her hospital stay. The access to her was controlled by Sasikala. There was a certain mystery about her illness because nobody had seen her during those seventy-five days when she was in the hospital. Even the health bulletins from the hospital were far and few. This resulted in a demand from the opposition parties, led by the DMK, that videos and pictures should be released to quell any rumours about her health, as was done in the case of MGR when he was hospitalised in 1984 but there was no response, which led to malicious rumours that Jaya was not alive. 'The DMK requested Governor Chennamaneni Vidyasagar Rao to take "due steps" in dispelling rumours even as the police filed a case against an "unknown person" for allegedly circulating rumours about the AIADMK supremo's condition. The case was filed under various sections of the

IPC, including those dealing with "public mischief" and "promoting enmity between classes".[92]

A team of medical experts from the All India Institute of Medical Sciences (AIIMS) was flown in from Delhi, as also an expert, Dr Richard John Beale, from London, to treat her, only in vain. Meanwhile, in October 2016, the Madras High Court directed Tamil Nadu's additional advocate general to get instructions from the government on her health, after social activist Ramaswamy filed a Public Interest Litigation seeking the real status of Jayalalithaa's health. The court also observed that people were anxious to know about the Chief Minister's health.

When the illness and her hospitalisation continued, she first shed her portfolios on October 11, to her Finance Minister O. Pannerselvam, who had stood in for her twice as Chief Minister. Two hours after the announcement of her death, in a swift political transition, Pannerselvam was sworn in as Chief Minister for the third time at a sombre ceremony at Raj Bhawan, along with all the ministers in the erstwhile Jayalalithaa cabinet to ensure smooth transfer of power. A team of officers were running the government from the hospital where they were stationed during the seventy-five days of her illness. The DMK demanded either a 'Chief Minister in-charge or a new Chief Minister,' to streamline governance. However, the demand failed to find support even from the key ally of the DMK- The Congress. On October 29, Jayalalithaa reportedly affixed her left thumb impression on the poll documents submitted by a AIADMK candidate, as her right hand was inflamed following a tracheostomy. By the first week of November, AIADMK claimed that Jayalalithaa would be discharged from the hospital.

In her first direct communication since her hospitalisation, Jayalalithaa said in a statement on November 13 that she had taken a rebirth because of people's prayers; she urged them to vote for the AIADMK in the November 19 polls. On November 25, the Apollo Hospital chairman Dr Pratap Reddy claimed that she was recovering, and that all her vital organs were functioning well. On December 4, Jayalalithaa suffered a severe cardiac arrest in the evening. The team of doctors from AIIMS was flown in once again, and on December 5, she was declared dead at midnight.

But how did she die? Why was there a mystery? Was it a mere lung infection? Was it fever and dehydration? Was it a multiple organ failure? Was it a severe and sudden cardiac arrest? Or was it something else like 'poisoning' that some critics allege? These were the questions raised in public. Two days before she suffered a massive cardiac arrest that led to her death, she was declared 'fully recovered' by a team of doctors who said she could decide when to go home.

Dr Richard Beale said in February 2017 that the former Tamil Nadu Chief Minister was critically ill, and that an acute sepsis led to her death. According to the *Economic Times*, he said in a press conference on February 6, organised with the help of the state Government, that there was no conspiracy, and no strange thing happened. This was done to alley the doubts raised about her health. Sasikala was under attack about why no one was allowed to see Jayalalithaa for seventy-five days when she was in the hospital.

Dr Richard Beale said 'She was admitted to hospital and was on the road to recovery but had a sudden cardiac arrest which led to her tragic death and this is what happened.'[93] However, some including the founder member of the AIADMK, P.H. Pandian, alleged that her death was unnatural. An expelled AIADMK Rajya Sabha member Sasikala Pushpa had moved the Supreme Court seeking a CBI probe or a judicial investigation by an apex court judge into the matter. A former Member of Parliament and film actress Gautami had written to the Prime Minister to investigate about the mystery. A Madras High Court judge S. Vaidyanathan, on hearing a petition on 29 December 2016 raised doubts over the death of Jayalalithaa while asking why her body can't be exhumed to understand the circumstances in which she died and the kind of treatment she was administered. TV channel News 18 reported that 'Since a few media outlets raised doubts, personally I too have my doubts. When she was admitted in hospital, it was told that she was on proper diet. After her death, at least now the truth should come out,' Justice S. Vaidyanathan said. The court had served notices to the Prime Minister's Office, Central ministries, the CBI, and Apollo Hospital over the issue.

This was taken forward further by Chief Minister O. Pannerselvam who had fallen out with Sasikala to announce a judicial probe by a High Court judge about the circumstances of Jaya's death, on 8 February 2017. In his first public comments on Jayalalithaa's hospitalisation, O. Pannerselvam said he could not meet her even once during her hospitalisation. 'For 75 days I went to the hospital. But I could not meet her even once. Even my family members used to ask me every day whether I met Amma. At one stage, I even thought of lying that I had met her. But I did not do so,' he told a Tamil TV channel. In short, there was secrecy, mystery, rumours and lies about the six-time Chief Minister Jayalalithaa's last days.

Jayalalithaa's popularity, not only in Tamil Nadu but also in the rest of the country, was evident when thousands of mourners went along the funeral procession to Marina beach where her body was buried near her mentor MGR's Samadhi, with full honours of a state funeral. The Prime Minister, President, Chief Ministers from at least eight states, ministers and other dignitaries arrived in Chennai to pay their last respects to the departed leader. While it was her 'sister' Sasikala who performed the last rites, Jaya's nephew Deepak was allowed to stand near her while niece Deepa was kept out. Though her nephew and niece were the only family left, Jayalalithaa did not keep in touch with them and they were kept away all her life just as she kept out her brother, Jayakumar. Jaya's forty-two-year-old niece, Deepa, was born in Jaya's Poes Garden residence and until the age of four lived with her aunt along with her parents. Jaya's relationship with her close and extended family deteriorated after she hosted the lavish wedding of her foster son V.N. Sudhakaran (who was disowned by her later) in September 1995. Deepa, who resembles Jayalalithaa, has emerged as a challenger to Sasikala by joining hands with Pannerselvam and other anti-Sasikala elements nursing political ambitions. She also contested from the prestigious R.K. Nagar Assembly constituency by-elections in Chennai against Sasikala's nephew T.T. V. Dinakaran. The seat fell vacant after the death of Jayalalithaa.

The Chicago-based World Federation of Tamil Youth, USA (WFOTY) held a memorial service for Jayalalithaa on 4 January 2017 at Capitol Hill in Washington D.C. This memorial service to India's Iron Lady, Amma, was well attended by community activists from across the US and Canada. This was claimed as the first ever memorial service for an Indian leader at Capitol Hill.

Jayalalithaa had said once: 'You see, for most of my life, I'd say for one third of my life I was entirely dominated by my mother. I'd do everything she wanted. I could never do anything I really wanted. Then for the other part of my life, I was entirely dominated by MGR. First I had to enter films for my mother's sake, and then I had to enter politics for MGR's sake. Now I am passing through my last phase of my life. Two thirds of my life is over, one third remains. I am living for myself.'[94] This third part, which she referred to, ended on 5 December 2016, at 11.20 p.m., when Jaya breathed her last and lost the biggest ever battle she fought. She died in Apollo Hospital in Chennai, where she was admitted on 22 September 2016 with complaints of fever and dehydration.

POSTSCRIPT

Jayalalithaa's death, at the age of sixty-eight, twenty-five years after she rode to power, has left a void, which is difficult to fill up. MGR, and after his death, Jayalalithaa, both played the anti-Karunanidhi-centric politics successfully.

Jaya succeeded MGR at the right time and carried on his legacy. Karunanidhi is now ninety-three and ailing, while his son, M.K. Stalin, has practically taken over the party as its working president, since January 2017. But in the case of the AIADMK, there is no strong leader to carry on the anti–DMK sentiments. Jaya's death might provide an opportunity for the national parties like the Congress, which lost power in 1967, and the BJP, which has not been able to find roots, to expand their base. Both the major Dravidian parties—the DMK and the AIADMK—continue to be relevant but they face the challenge of overcoming the present confusion after the death of Jayalalithaa. The real strength of AIADMK has been Jayalalithaa's connect with the people whereas other political parties, especially the DMK, have their own dedicated cadre with clear lines of succession. It is doubtful whether the party can remain united in future unless some strong leader emerges.

As *The Hindu* editorial on 7 December 2016, said: 'Adversity brought out the best in Jayalalithaa. As the Chief

Minister fighting for the rights of her state, as a politician trying to spring back from electoral defeats, as a woman standing up to sexist taunts in what is still very much a man's world, she was courageous to the point of being adventurist. In her passing, India has lost a leader who played a vital role in the shaping of Tamil Nadu during a crucial phase of the country's economic development and social progress.'

LARGER THAN LIFE

Jayalalithaa has left behind a rich legacy in political, administrative, economic and welfare areas. She was hailed as a good administrator. The *New York Times* notes that , 'Jean Drèze and Amartya Sen, in their book *An Uncertain Glory,* an analysis of economic development in India, single out Tamil Nadu as a paragon of administrative innovation among Indian states, ranking it best in the country for the quality of its public services. Under Jayalalithaa and Karunanidhi's governance, Chennai has gained a reputation as the Detroit of India (in the car-manufacturing-hub sense, not in the bankrupt-and-abandoned sense). Her raw instinct for political survival was enough to put her in office. Once there, she revealed a surprising talent for administration.'[95]

Jayalalithaa has also left a legacy of public policy that encourages welfare measures like the distribution of many subsidised commodities such as rice under the Public Distribution System (PDS), laptops, bicycles, books, notebooks, mid-day meals to school children and highly-subsidised electricity tariffs, to name a few. She also promised mopeds to working women, mobiles to members of self-help groups, etc. Sustaining such largesse from the state would be a challenge for the new government.

She had deeply invested in her image as the benefactor of the masses. This acquired image made her immune to all other criticism. It didn't matter if the freebees bearing her pictures were of sub-standard quality and were channelled into the market at huge discounts. The image was everything and was micromanaged ruthlessly. After all, politics is perception; and in the perception war, she won. Moreover, defeat never demoralised her because she knew that that was the way politics worked.

During her first term, from 1991-96, she was keen to learn and provide good governance. When she took over, most things went in her favour as she was fresh, intelligent, political and understood the nuances of Tamil Nadu politics. But somewhere she lost her way and began to indulge in opulence, thereby losing sight of good governance. She became arrogant and a megalomaniac, and would not listen to a 'no' from her officers. At the same time, bureaucrats who worked with her claim that she was quite decisive and her orders were clear and specific. She expected them to implement her decisions faithfully and would not tolerate any defiance. In every ministry, she appointed a person who she trusted, and worked through them; they were her eyes and ears. Her bureaucrats had the upper hand in telling ministers what to do, and she relied on their channels to report any excesses to her. Even in cabinet meetings, no minister could question her as they were afraid to lose their jobs if they did so. The cabinet meetings lasted for just enough time for them to okay each item.

The issue of Sri Lankan Tamils was close to her heart. After the UK-based Channel 4 broadcasted an image of the Sri Lankan army distributing chocolates after killing LTTE Chief Prabhakaran's teenage son, Balachandran, there was a students' unrest in Tamil Nadu. In support, she called off the 20th Asian Athletics Championships scheduled to be held in Chennai in July 2013, saying that the Sri Lankan players had no place in the state. The heat generated by the Tamil Nadu youth, besides the Diaspora, also compelled the Tamil Nadu government to pass resolutions urging the Centre to stop calling Sri Lanka a 'friendly nation', and the Assembly demanded that an independent international inquiry be conducted into 'genocide' and 'war crimes' committed in the final phase of the Eelam war 4 in 2009; those found guilty be produced before an international court and given appropriate punishment; and till the Sri Lankan government stopped repression of Tamils, an economic embargo be imposed on the island nation. She led the Dravidian parties in putting pressure on Prime Minister Manmohan Singh to skip the Commonwealth Heads of Government Meeting (CHOGM) held in Colombo in November 2013. She used the Sri Lankan issue to expose the double speak of Karunanidhi, who was the Chief Minister when the Eelam War 4 ended on 18 May, 2009. She even discussed the Sri Lankan problem with the US Secretary of state, Hillary Clinton, when the latter visited Chennai to meet her in 2011.

Did Jaya develop an aura around herself as a shield? She claimed that it was not something she consciously did and she was just trying to be herself. 'So in order to be able to run such a party successfully and steer it to victory, you got to be tough, you got to be strong, many times you have to be ruthless, you also have to be compassionate, you also have to be considerate. I am all of these things. But more importantly, unless you are strong and tough and a 100 times more suitable if you happen to be a woman, you just can't cope with the pressures of a political career, you just can't govern a state, you can't administer the state well unless you are strong and tough. So I have to be strong, I have to be tough and when I run my party successfully and when I give a good administration, instead of appreciating my performance, people say "Oh! She is tough, she is autocratic, she is dictatorial and so on and so forth." If I had not been any of these things, if I had given a weak inefficient administration, if I would not have been able to keep a grip on my party, they would have said she is a failure because she is a woman. That's it.' [96]

A Wikileaks telegram describes her performance on Tamil Nadu economy thus: 'Jayalalithaa, who took office just as India began to open its economy, has been described by business executives and AIADMK sources as a "pro-business" politician who is "friendly" to multinational corporations. She worked to bring foreign investors to Tamil Nadu, laying the groundwork for big-ticket projects by Ford, DuPont, and Hyundai. Many Indian business leaders have told post that although the AIADMK and DMK are both corrupt, they prefer Jayalalithaa because her AIADMK is more efficient at delivering once paid. Centralization of power in the AIADMK means that things move quickly once Jayalalithaa gets her cut: her subordinates snap to attention when she approves a project. "If I pay her, I know my job will get done," one contact told post, "but with the DMK you can pay Karunanidhi and another ten guys will still come asking for more." International businesses also appreciate Jayalalithaa's excellent convent-educated English speaking ability, which stands in stark contrast to the majority of Tamil Nadu politicians who have very limited English skills.'[97]

A peculiar thing in Tamil Nadu, right from the days of MGR, was that the administration could run without the Chief Minister going to the Secretariat; and Jayalalithaa carried it forward. She would rarely visit Fort St George because the administration ran on auto-pilot.

She would often write letters to the Prime Ministers pertaining to the important issues of the state. She led the

Assembly in passing resolutions against the Sri Lankan President Rajapakse after the end of the 2009 Eelam War IV. She would not allow the Centre to meddle with the Officers of the state. She kept aside her friendship with Prime Minister Narendra Modi in 2016 and submitted a memorandum about her reasons for opposing the Goods and Services Tax (GST) and also the implementation of the Food Security Act. On 15 June 2016, when Jayalalithaa visited New Delhi, she explained why she was opposing the GST. 'Tamil Nadu is concerned about the impact the proposed GST will have on the fiscal autonomy of states and the huge permanent revenue loss it is likely to cause to a manufacturing and net exporting state like Tamil Nadu,' Jayalalithaa said in a memorandum to the Prime Minister.[98] Noting that a manufacturing state like Tamil Nadu would permanently lose substantial revenue (estimated loss of Rs 9,270 crores) if GST is implemented, she reiterated the need for a constitutionally mandated independent compensation mechanism for full (100 per cent) compensation of revenue losses suffered by the state for a period of not less than five years.

Journalist T.S. Subramaniam points out that 'she performed somersaults on crucial issues such as the Sri Lankan Tamils' cause, the first nuclear power reactor going critical in the Kudankulam Nuclear Power Project, and the Gas Authority of India Limited's pipeline project in the state. On April 16, 2002, the Assembly adopted a resolution urging the Centre to send the Army to Sri Lanka, with the consent of Colombo, to capture Velupillai Prabhakaran, the leader of the Liberation Tigers of Tamil Eelam, and bring him to stand trial in the Rajiv Gandhi assassination case. In February 2014, with an eye on the Lok Sabha elections, the Jayalalithaa cabinet decided to release from prison all the seven accused (Murugan, Nalini, Perarivalan, Santhan,

Robert Payas, Jayakumar and Ravichandran) in the Rajiv Gandhi case under Section 435 of the Code of Criminal Procedure. The Cabinet's decision was forwarded to the Centre. In March 2016, ahead of the Assembly elections, the Jayalalithaa government made another attempt to release the seven convicted persons and wrote to the Centre seeking its views on the decision. The Centre rejected the Tamil Nadu proposal in April 2016.'[99]

SHOES TOO BIG TO FILL

There was chaos and confusion after the death of Jayalalithaa. Since she had not groomed anyone as her successor, the party was confused about who should take over her mantle. Her mentor MGR, too, had not named his successor. Jaya did not leave behind a will even for her personal assets. In an affidavit filed before the Election Commission in 2016, she had declared her assets at a conservative value of Rs 118.58 crores. Except the Poes Garden bungalow and some inherited jewelry, a special court had attached all these properties in the Disproportionate Assets case. She also had deposits of Rs 10.63 crores in banks, and 1,250 kgs of silver apart from the gold and silver seized by the court.

A source close to Jayalalithaa maintains that she believed in astrology, and that it was predicted that she would live up to eighty years. Perhaps she might have thought there was no hurry to name a successor or leave a will. The other theory is that like her mentor, she, too, thought that 'After me the deluge' because she could not bring herself to believe that anyone could match her. She may have even thought that after her death, the party would choose the best among those who were competing for her legacy. She followed the policy of many other dictators who did not name their successors. In any case, her death has resulted in a power struggle within the party. It is common knowledge that Jaya often consulted astrologers. *India Today* magazine points out that she added an extra 'a' to her name Jayalalitha. 'The name change was attributed to a yagna that she performed a year ago to goddess Kali at a temple in Thanjavur. The yagna was performed with the aim of coming back to power, which she did in the 2001-assembly elections and then the journalists were asked to spell her name with 12 characters instead of 11—from Jayalalitha to Jayalalithaa.'[100] If she launched any scheme, she would consult astrologers for an exact and auspicious time and date.

SASIKALA TAKES OVER

Jayalalithaa's death has brought Sasikala, Jaya's close aide, companion, long-time shadow, and a woman whom she called her sister and also her alter ego, to the forefront. Who is Sasikala and why was she important to Jaya? Little is known about Sasikala's early life except that she is from Mannargudi in Tamil Nadu's Tiruvarur district. She hails from the Kallar community, a sub-caste of the powerful Thevar community. In 1975, she married Chennai-based M. Natarajan, then an Assistant Public Relations officer. She was a school dropout but ambitious. It was V.S. Chandralekha, the Cuddalore district collector who introduced Sasikala, who was running a video rental shop, to Jayalalithaa in the early eighties. She became close to Jayalalithaa and later on, her confidante. Sasikala was little heard and hardly seen but she became powerful in the party and government affairs. She helped all her family members and her family became very rich by the time Jayalalithaa completed her first term. The stories of alleged money-making by Sasikala's family members spread across the state. As the friendship between the two women grew, so did the fortunes of Sasikala's community, which soon had a foothold in every layer of the government and the party. The AIADMK and Jaya benefitted from the consolidation of the Thevar community's vote bank, politically.

Jayalalithaa even adopted Sasikala's nephew V.M. Sudhakaran as her foster son and his marriage to Tamil actor Sivaji Ganesan's grand-daughter Satyavati saw the Chief Minister splurging crores on a wedding that holds the Guinness World Record for maximum number of guests at a wedding, and for the largest banquet. The other nephew, Dinakaran, was made a Member of Parliament.

As *Business Standard* notes, 'By 1991, when Jayalalithaa became Chief Minister, Sasikala was her most trusted confidante. She had moved into Jaya's Poes Garden house in 1989 along with an army of 40 servants that included maids, security guards, drivers and cooks. All of them came from Sasikala's hometown, Manargudi. Several of Sasikala's relatives also moved in. Others, like her brother, his wife, nieces and in-laws, became frequent visitors.' A 2012 report described her role in Jayalalithaa's life as that of a 'soul mate, housekeeper, and political confidante. And a tremendous but unelected power centre.'[101] It adds that she would be present at Jayalalithaa's meetings with the visiting dignitaries, serve them food, take calls on projects and attend Jayalalithaa's meetings with the ministers. More importantly, she also controlled the access to Jayalalithaa.

However, there were murmurs in the party about the dominance of Sasikala's family. 'During the AIADMK regime of 2001-2006, it was alleged that most government contracts went to businessmen close to the family. Again in the run-up to the May 2011 Assembly polls, the Sasikala clan decided who would get the party ticket and seat sharing. The family allegedly planted its men in key positions in the government so much so that it was suspected that they wanted to keep a watch on Jayalalithaa's each administrative move.'[102]

Though Jayalalithaa lost power in 1996, she did well in 1998 by becoming a partner with the BJP in Lok Sabha polls.

Sasikala's family continued to flourish after that because the AIADMK was a partner in the Vajpayee government. When the BJP managers in Delhi side-lined Sasikala, it was alleged that it was she who was instrumental in Jayalalithaa joining hands with the Congress to bring down the Vajpayee government. After that, when Jaya came back to power in 2001, the family had acquired more clout.

Jayalalithaa threw Sasikala out on two occasions, only to get her back after a few weeks. The first was after Jayalalithaa's defeat in the Assembly polls in 1996, when the party felt that it was because of Sasikala's dominance that the AIADMK lost the elections, Jayalalithaa banished her only to get her back within few weeks after Sasikala wrote letters pleading ignorance about the corruption charges.

The friendship hit a bump again in 2011, shortly after the AIADMK swept to power in the Assembly elections. One day, she suddenly announced the ouster of Sasikala, her husband and twelve others from the party's primary membership. 'No reason was given for the action. But reports suggested a suspected "palace coup" being planned by Sasikala and her family against Jayalalithaa. There were also unconfirmed reports that Jayalalithaa was being given small quantities of sedatives and harmful chemicals to harm her.[103] But the two patched up within weeks with Sasikala giving an open apology. In an emotional letter, Sasikala claimed that 'Not even in my wildest dreams I have thought of betraying Jayalalithaa... I have no ambitions either in the party or the government... and anyone who conspired against 'Akka' (elder sister) will remain persona non grata to me.' It is a mystery why Jayalalithaa could not part with Sasikala for long. In her last days, it was Sasikala who controlled access to Jayalalithaa and it was Sasikala who played the main part in her cremation.

Jaya's faith in Sasikala was unshakable. She once claimed that, 'Sasikala is a much misunderstood maligned person. And she has been the target of a lot of vilification and persecution simply because of her loyalty to me and her closeness to me. If it had not been her friendship with me, no one would have attacked her in the way she has been attacked. You know, she had to spend nearly a year in prison. She has suffered a lot. Most of the criticism has come from men, men who are politicians too. You see, it is impossible for someone who is in the thick of politics to run a political career and manage a household. But most men don't understand this because they have their women at home. They have their wives or mothers to look after their personal needs. Now for example, I can't go out shopping. Someone has to do my shopping for me. And I have to leave at odd times, I have to leave in a hurry. There's no time for me to lock up the house or to see that everything is safely put away. I just can't attend to these practical things. Someone has to manage things for me. She does all that. So she to me is the sister I never had. And she has taken my mother's place, she looks after me. There are many who think it would be useful to them to be in her place. So these are the people who created all these nasty stories about her. Because they tried to separate her from me and tried to worm their way into my good books and tried to get into the place that she occupies but they didn't succeed.'[104]

Sasikala had been with Jaya in her good times and bad times. She was a co-accused in most of the cases Jaya was facing in courts. So when Jayalalithaa died, the party clung to 'Chinnamma' as they thought she could be the uniting factor. It was an emotional moment. This was because Jayalalithaa did not develop a second or even third line of leadership. And though Sasikala is said to have interacted with ministers on a regular basis, even deciding candidates during elections and taking part in alliance negotiations, she has never had a public political profile. Jayalalithaa never gave her any official position or made her a minister or an office bearer in the party or hinted that Sasikala would take over after her death.

Sasikala came out in the open for the first time when Jayalalithaa's body was kept at the Rajaji Hall on 6 December 2016 for the public to pay their homage. In fact, Sasikala and her family members, who had been banned by Jaya in 2011, had positioned themselves near the body, which put off the cadres. Sasikala also performed the last rites of the departed leader on the Marina beach.

Sasikala did not wait for long to take over the party. Soon after Jaya's demise, in carefully orchestrated events, AIADMK Members of Parliament, youth wing office-bearers, information technology wing members, office-bearers of various districts, and leaders of various caste outfits, made a beeline for Poes Garden to plead with Sasikala to become the general secretary in an orchestrated manner. Chief Minister Pannerselvam also joined the chorus, which was led by Deputy Speaker of Lok Sabha Thambi Durai. They did so because Sasikala held the purse strings of the party. Also, most of them owed their position in the party or the government to Sasikala, and they wanted to show their loyalty to her. At any cost, no MLA wanted to contest elections again with four-and-a-half years left for the next polls. Also, they did not know who would get them elected as Jaya was no more.

If Sasikala thought that it would be smooth sailing for her to succeed Jayalalithaa, she found it the hard way that it was not that easy. While Chief Minister Pannerselvam went along with her initially by proposing her name as the powerful general secretary of the party, a post held by Jaya all along, he fell out with her when Sasikala tried to oust him and become the Chief Minister. Sasikala's supporters argued that *aatchi* (government) and *katchi* (party) should be controlled by the same person and she should take charge both as the general secretary as well as Chief Minister. Pannerselvam dropped a bombshell forty-eight hours after proposing Sasikala's name to succeed him as Chief Minister. On 7 February 2017, around 10 p.m., he went to Jayalalithaa's Samadhi at Marina beach and opened the revolt against Sasikala. He made a dramatic disclosure that she had forced him to resign from his post on February 5. He was also forced to propose Sasikala's name in the legislators' meeting on the same day. In an unusual manner, Pannerselvam declared that 'I am laying these facts in front of you to make things clear in public, I will continue to struggle.' He prayed before Jayalalithaa's Samadhi for forty minutes and at the end of it calmly declared his intention to revolt, hinting he had some backing in the party, and that he was willing to take back his resignation if the cadres supported him. Narrating how he was humiliated by Sasikala and her family after the death of Jayalalithaa, he noted that he was undermined time and again and was made to sit in the front row and not on the dais in meetings, even though he was the Chief Minister. The AIADMK went for a horizontal split, with Pannerselvam parting ways with Sasikala. He became the magnet for the other disgruntled elements in the party.

Interestingly, the legislature party meeting to elect Sasikala as its leader was convened after the Madras High Court refused on 1 February 2017 to discharge her from three Foreign Exchange Regulation Act violation cases filed by the Enforcement Directorate (ED). The court refused to discharge her from three cases filed by the Enforcement Directorate in 1995 and 1996 on charges of violating the Foreign Exchange Regulation Act (1973), for cases related to payments made in US and Singapore dollars to foreign firms for hiring transponders and uplink facilities for the J.J. TV (which later became Jaya TV.) Moreover, her elevation as the party general secretary was also questioned by her detractors. As per the party constitution, a general secretary has to be elected by all primary members and not just by those who constitute the general council. This rule was brought in by party founder MGR in the Eighties and was retained by Jayalalithaa. Thus, while AIADMK leaders declared her the general secretary, a formal election with the concurrence of every level of the organisation structure had not taken place. Moreover, while the MPs and MLAs supported her, the cadre did not fully support her. The case is pending before the Election Commission, which has frozen the two leaves symbol.

But Sasikala's plan to get hastily sworn in failed after Governor C. Vidyasagar Rao delayed the swearing-in, keeping in view the hints from the Supreme Court that it would pronounce within a week the verdict on the Disproportionate Assets case. Although the Karnataka High Court had acquitted Jaya and her aides, the Apex court had not yet cleared her. Moreover, there was public outcry against Sasikala taking over the party through the backdoor as they voted for Jayalalithaa in the 2016 elections and not for her. There were also apprehensions that her family, which is called 'Mannargudi mafia', would capture the party and the government. Her detractors pointed out that she had exposed herself as power hungry. In comparison, Pannerselvam came across as a better human being and administrator. It was like the proverbial slip between the cup and the lip.

The verdict from the court, which came on 14 February practically ended Sasikala's political ambitions. The two-judge bench held by Justice P.C. Ghosh and Justice Amitava

Roy delivered its reserved judgment (since June 2016) against Jayalalithaa, Sasikala, her sister-in-law Ilavarasi, and her nephew Sudhakaran. Restoring the Bengaluru trial court's conviction order, it set aside 'in toto' the Karnataka High Court judgment that acquitted all four in 2015. They convicted and sentenced Sasikala to four years' imprisonment for conspiring with and abetting Jayalalithaa's 'sinister' design to 'launder ill-gotten wealth' to the tune of Rs 53.6 crores. The apex court observed, 'Although all the accused claimed to have independent sources of income but the fact of constitution of firms and acquisition of large tracts of land out of the funds provided by A1 (Jayalalithaa) indicate that, they congregated in the house of A1 neither for social living nor Jaya allowed her free accommodation out of humanitarian concern, rather the facts and circumstances proved in evidence undoubtedly point out that they were accommodated in the house of A1 pursuant to the criminal conspiracy hatched by them to hold the assets of A1.'[105]

What dashed Sasikala's hopes at this point of time was that the judgment barred her from contesting elections for at least ten years, four years of jail term and then another six years. It also referred to the statement of a prosecution witness and observed that Jayalalithaa had issued a blanket instruction that directions issued by Sasikala from time to time ought to be followed; consequently she was to decide in which account the huge deposits were to be made. Jayalalithaa had executed a general power of attorney in Sasikala's favour.

Sasikala had no other option than to surrender and go to jail in Parappana Agraharam, in Bengaluru where she will have to serve her sentence for the next four years. This was the third jail sentence for her as she had been in jail on two other occasions when Jayalalithaa was sent to the prison.

Learning a lesson or two from Jayalalithaa, Sasikala chalked out a strategy to deal with the situation. The first thing she did was to choose a proxy Chief Minister who could be controlled by her from prison. She selected Edappadi Palaniswamy and also ensured that the flock remained with her and voted for him by keeping them in a luxury resort near Chennai. Having sorted out the issue of governance, she turned her attention to the party. She chose her nephew Dinakaran and appointed him as the deputy general secretary to control the party even while her own elevation is under question by the Election Commission. Jayalalithaa had expelled him from the party in 2011, but Sasikala admitted him and another relative, Dr Venkatesh, the day before she surrendered before the trial court, making it clear that it will be the Mannargudi clan, which will be in control. In fact, Dinakaran was also assigned to oversee the governance and breathe over the shoulders of Palaniswamy. There was no doubt in anybody's mind that the party and the government had been high jacked from right under their noses.

While the story of Jaya had ended with her death, Sasikala's dramatic rise to power and her end in prison is a continuing story. Jaya has left behind an enduring legacy with benevolent welfare measures for the common man, especially the women, and these are remembered and cherished by the masses who helped her come back to power. While Jayalalithaa was able to fill the vacuum after her mentor MGR's death, and took the party forward by making it the third largest party in Parliament, Sasikala, who took over the reins after Jayalalithaa's demise has had the misfortune to go to jail for four years. Moreover, Sasikala has no charisma or public face and what little is known about her in the public domain is not appreciated. Therefore, the party nurtured for decades by MGR and Jayalalithaa had to split.

As *India Today* notes: 'She (Jayalalithaa) has allowed rumour and secrecy to define her life, cultivating it deliberately as part of her aura. She is admired for her courage and worshipped for the power she wields and, at the same time, exploited by the circumstances of her loneliness. She is nobody's fool and far from being the stereotypical film heroine of her time, fought against her own destiny to emerge as a success in public life. This despite the exploitation and suffering she had to endure in the Tamil film industry and at the hands of her mentor M.G. Ramachandran.'[106]

Jayalalithaa used to allocate huge amounts of money for the renovation of temples. Though belonging to a Dravidian party, she herself did not hesitate to visit temples or remain a practicing Hindu. Her mentor, MGR, would also visit the Mookambikai temple in Karnataka. There is now a proposal to build a temple for Jaya in Iyeppedu village, sixty kilometres from Vellore, by the end of 2017. The decision to build the temple was taken even when she was alive. According to a Zee News report, 'This temple is the brainchild of 37 year old A.P. Srinivasan. An active member of the AIADMK, Srinivasan is the MGR youth wing joint secretary of Virugampakkam constituency. This temple will on a 1200 sq. feet of land owned by him in Iyeppedu village, 60 kilometers from Vellore and is estimated to cost Rs 50 lakhs. Amma Alayam will house a six foot tall bronze statue of Jayalalithaa, besides showcasing her life and achievements.'[107]

Another temple for the departed Chief Minister was built ten days after her death, by the AIADMK councilor M. Swaminathan. The temple was built at a cost of Rs 2 lakhs. He said, 'We have kept a big picture of Amma inside in which she is seen sitting on a big throne. Photos of Annadurai and MGR are also there.'[108] Devotees will also be taken down the memory lane, as pictures of Jayalalithaa, right from her childhood to her last days, will be put up on the temple's exterior walls. There are also plans to erect a statue of Jayalalithaa.

Jayalalihtaa is now dead. Her companion Sasikala is languishing in jail and has no future for at least the next ten years. The party has split. Sasikala's nominee and the present Chief Minsiter E. Palaniswamy has no credibility. Sasikala's nephew Dinakaran, to whom Sasikala has entrusted the party, also has no credibility.

Two months after Sasikala installed her puppet Chief Minister E.Palaniswamy and anointed her nephew T.T.V.Dinakaran as the Deputy general secretary of the AIADMK, things took a dramatic turn. Sasikala was unable to control the party from jail although Dinakaran was visiting her frequently. Her lust for power made her choose Dinakaran to contest from the R.K.Nagar constituency bye elections which had fallen vacant after the death of Jayalalihtaa. The election was scheduled to be held on April 12. The Pannerselvam camp had put up the old warhorse Madhusudanan, who was the chariman of the united AIADMK Presidium while Jaya's niece Deepa Jayakumar also contested the polls on her own. Since the Election Commission had frozen the two leaves symbol, the two factions contested on other symbols. Sasikala's plan was that Dinakaran should become the chief minsiter after winning the polls. For this purpose Sasikala and her nephew were alleged to have spent a lot of money by offering bribes to the voters. On complaints from the other faction and the DMK, the Election Commission entered the picture and at the instance of the Commission, the Income Tax department conduced raids in various places including the residence of an AIADMK Health minister C.Vijaya Bhaskar and people close to him in 35 places across the state and recovered crores of rupess as well as evidence of voter list and who should be given money. The Election Commission then decided to postpone the poll on April 11, a day before the polls were scheduled. That was not all. Perhaps not wanting to leave any stone unturned, Dinakaran foolishly had allegedly used a middleman who confessed to the police that Dinakran had made a deal with him for Rs 50 crores to get the two leaves symbol freed by bribing the Election Commission officials so that the Dinakaran faction could use it. The Commission had frozen the symbol after both Pannerselvam and Sasikala factions staked claim to it ahead of the now countermanded April 12 bye elections to R.K.Nagar Assembly constituency. The symbol was identified with MGR and Jayalalihtaa and it was important to get the symbol. Chandrashekhar had allegedly told Dinakaran that his contacts in the Commission could help the Sasikala faction to get the two leaves poll symbol ahead of R.K.Nagar bye elections.

The middleman Sukesh Chandrashekhar was arrested in Delhi following which the Delhi police decided to go to Chennai and investigate the case. This has made the Sasikala faction jittery and even the ministers got nervous with the result they had decided to ditch Chinnamma and her nephew. As if on cue there were efforts for a patch up between the Palaniswamy and Panneerselvam factions. It suited Palaniswamy to join hands with Pannerselvam as he feared that Dinakaran might sideline him once he became a legislator. Pannerselvam claimed that he had won the first round because his condition for the unity move was to keep the 'Mannargudi mafia (Sasikala and Dinakaran) out' which had been accepted by the EPS faction. AIADMK Minister Jayakumar told the media after a crucial meeting of the ministers, which decided to dump Chinnamma and her nephew "The decision to merge was to ensure that the

party did not break. The party should stand united.........
The move to sideline the Sasikala clan was to ensure that
the party and the government did not fall into the hands
of one family."[109] While Sasikala found it difficult to keep
her flock together and Dinakaran getting into more and
more problems, there was no other option for both Sasikala
and Dinakaran to resign to their fate when the two factions
came together on April 18. Pressure was already building
up on Dinakaran to step down after the cancellation of the
R.K.Nagar polls. By dumping them the two factions felt that
they were washing away the Chinnamma taint. Dinakaran
had given Pannerselvam the opening he needed to emerge
as a strong candidate and consolidate his position in the
party and the government. His patience and caution seems
to have borne fruit. While Pannerselvam lost the first
round to Sasikala when she snatched his chief minister's
post in February, he managed to win the second round by
winning his condition to keep the Mannargudi mafia away.
"We, which include the chief minister, ministers, MLAs,
MPs, district secretries, headquarters office bearers, grass
root level office bearers, have come together and took a
unanimous decision to keep Dinakaran and family away
from the party affairs. This is a wish of the 1.5 crore party
cadre. We have decided to keep the Sasikala family away
from party affairs."[110] Both factions have proved that power
is the only glue that matters and not loyalty. No matter how
bitter the factionalism, the legislators in the two factions do
not want to fight elections when there are four more years
to go. By dumping the aunt and the nephew Palaniswamy
also wanted to endear himself to the Centre.

The BJP had been wooing the United AIADMK for
almost a decade. So it will be happy to deal with a united
party. The realisation that Sasikala was not popular and her
influence did not go beyond some legislators and people

hated her followed by a split was an obvious worry for the BJP. A reunited AIADMK minus the Sasikala clan would be ethically and electorally acceptable to the BJP. It is of course a question mark whether the united AIADMK will be cohesive as there is no single leader who can keep the party united. Although things seem to be on the mend, the AIADMK's future does not appear to be bright. In 1989, the faction led by Jayalalithaa and another by Janaki Ramachandran, both vying to be the successor to the iconic Chief Minister M. G. Ramachandran, set aside their bitter rivalry to create a united AIADMK – a party that went on to dominate Tamil Nadu politics for over two and half decades there is no such charismatic leader in sight now. In a way if the party does not survive it is a failure of Jayalalithaa's vision to ensure the continuance of the party. Jayalalithaa may be dead, but the people of Tamil Nadu will not forget her despite all her faults. She has ensured that her legend lives on forever. She was an empress when alive, and is certainly an empress in death.

ENDNOTES

1   Annie Gowen, 'Jayalalihtaa Jayaram, powerful Indian politician who broke gender barriers dies at 68', *Washington Post*, 5 December 2016.

2   Wikileaks, 'Women in India: Tamil Nadu's iron lady J. Jayalalithaa', 19 March 2009.

3   Wikileaks, Chennai to CIA telegram no 09CHENNAI81_a, 19 March 2009.

4   Author's interview with Dr Subramanian Swamy.

5   Interview with Rajat Sharma, *Aap Ki Adalat*, updated telecast on India TV on 14 May 2011.

6   Interview with Rajat Sharma, *Aap Ki Adalat*, updated telecast on India TV on 14 May 2011.

7   Ibid.

8   Ibid.

9   Online Desk, 'I don't think anyone has taken more criticism than I: Jaya told Simi Garewal', *The New Indian Express*, 6 December 2016.

10   Online Desk, 'I don't think anyone has taken more criticism than I: Jaya told Simi Garewal, *The New Indian Express*, 6 December 2016.

11   Ibid.

12   Author's interview with Kumar.

13   Author's interview with Kartikeyan.

14   Online Desk, 'I don't think anyone has taken more criticism than I: Jaya told Simi Garewal', *The New Indian Express*, 6 December 2016.

15   Author's interview with Tirunavukkarasu.

16   Ajit Pillai, 'The life and times of Jayalalitha', *Outlook*, May 1998.

17   Online Desk, 'I don't think anyone has taken more criticism than I: Jaya told Simi Garewal', *The New Indian Express*, 6 December 2016.

18   Ibid.

19   Kalyani Shankar, *Gods of Power*, (Macmillan India, New Delhi, 2000, p. 87.)

20   K. Mohandas, *MGR: The Man and The Myth*, Panther Publishers, Bengaluru, 1992.

21   Ibid.

22   Ibid.

23   Author's interview with N. Ravi.

24   Author's interview with Mani Shankar Aiyar.

25   Smriti Kak Ramachandran, 'Indira Gandhi came to hear Jayalalithaa's speech, recalls Kurien', *The Hindustan Times*, 6 December 2016.

26   K. Mohandas, *MGR: The Man and The Myth*, Panther Publishers, Bengaluru, 1992.

27   Internet Desk, (article*) 'Jayalalihtaa: A political career with sharp rises and steep falls', The Hindu*, 6, December 2016

28   ibid.

29   Ibid

30   Author's interview with Tirunavukkarasu.

31   Ajit Pillai, 'The life and times of Jayalalithaa', *Outlook*, 4 May 1998.

32   Author's interview with Tirunavukkarasu.

33   K. Mohandas, *MGR: The Man and The Myth*, Panther Publishers, Bengaluru, 1992.

34 Prabhu Chawla, 'I will carry the message', *India Today*, 15 January 1988.

35 Interview with Rajat Sharma, *Aap Ki Adalat*, updated telecast on India TV on 14 May 2011.

36 Author's interview with Jana Krishnamurthy.

37 R. Venkataraman, *My Presidential Years*, South Asia Books, 1994.

38 M. Karunanidhi, *Nenjukku Needi*, Thirumagal Nilayam, Chennai, 1997 June

39 Author's interview with G.K. Moopnar.

40 Online Desk, 'I don't think anyone has taken more criticism than I: Jaya told Simi Garewal', *The New Indian Express*, 6 December 2016.

41 Ibid.

42 Ibid.

43 Author's interview with Tirunavukkarasu.

44 Author's interview with G.K. Moopanar.

45 Author's interview with Dr Subramanian Swamy

46 http/wikileaks.org/cable/2009/03./Chennai181.html.

47 Stephan David, 'Death of an outlaw', *India Today*, 5 November 2011.

48 Author's interview with Bhishma Narain Singh.

49 Ibid.

50

51 Ibid.

52 Ibid.

53 Interview with Rajat Sharma, *Aap Ki Adalat*, updated telecast on India TV on 14 May 2011.

54 Author's interview with Tirunavukkarasu.

55 Author's interview with Bhishma Narain Singh.

56 Author's interview with Dr Subramanian Swamy.

57 Prakash M. Swamy, 'Jayalalithaa on the warpath', *India Today*, 31 January 1991.

58 Author's interview with P.V. Narasimha Rao.

59   Author's interview with P.V.Narasimha Rao.

60   Dhrubo Jyoti, 'Not Amma to all: The other side of Jayalalithaa's legacy', *The Hindustan Times*, 8 December 2016.

61   Kalyani Shankar, *Gods of Power*, Macmillan India, New Delhi, updated edition, 2005, p 111.

62   Author's interview with G.K. Moopanar.

63   M.R.Venkatesh, 'Rajni's revenge on traffic stopper Jaya', *The Telegraph*, 12 March 2008.

64   Prabhu Chawla, 'There is no alternative to Jayalalithaa', *India Today*, 28 November 2005.

65   Ibid.

66   Author's interview with Jana Krishnamurthy.

67   Barry Bearack, 'India's coalition is teetering as ex-actress pushes demands', *New York Times*, 5 April 1999.

68   Author's interview with Dr Subramanian Swamy.

69   Ibid.

70   Ibid.

71   Author's interview with T.V.R. Shenoy.

72   Ceilia W. Duger, 'Fiery actress strengthens opposition role in India', *New York Times*, 13 May 2001.

73   Online Desk, 'I don't think anyone has taken more criticism than I: Jaya told Simi Garewal', *The New Indian Express*, 6 December 2016.

74   Prabhu Chawla, 'There is no alternative to Jayalalithaa', *India Today*, 28 November 2005.

75   Wikileaks, Chennai to CIA telegram no 09CHENNAI81_a, 19 March 2009.

76   Arvindan Neelakandan, 'When Jayalalithaa faced tough opposition against her anti conversion bill 2002', *The Swarajya*, 8 December 2016.

77   Ibid.

78   Wikileaks, 'Women in India: Tamil Nadu's iron lady J. Jayalalithaa', 19 March 2009.

79 Jayaraj Sivam, 'Three little words no bureaucrat in Jayalalithaa's government wanted to hear', *The Times of India*, 5 December 2016.

80 M.K. Narayanan, 'The Jayalalithaa mystique', *The Hindu*, 21 December 2016.

81 'Chennai' Jayalalihtaa turns Rs 1200 crore new secretariat into hospital', *India Today*, 19 August 2011.

82 N. Madhavan, 'Jaya gets a clear mandate but faces a daunting task', IANS report, 13 May 2011.

83 Press Trust of India, 'Clinton, Jayalalihtaa discuss current situation in Sri Lanka, 'July 23, 2011.

84 Banyan, 'Jayalalithaa's gambit', *The Economist*, 6 September 2012.

85 'Presidential polls: Jayalalithaa asks political parties to back P.A. Sangma as presidential candidate', PTI report, 18 May 2012.

86 Vinay Kumar Ramakrishna, 'Jayalalithaa steps campaign for Sangma', *The Hindu*, 20 May 2012.

87 'Jayalalithaa strives to achieve double digit industrial growth in coming years', Millennium post, 22 February 2014.

88 K.M. Rakesh, 'Acquitted Amma's Jaya day', *The Telegraph* 12 May 2015.

89 Nirupama Subramanian, 'Win it like Jayalalithaa', *The Indian Express*, 21 May 2016.

90 Special Correspondent, 'Jayalalihtaa thanks Wigneswaran,' *The Hindu*, 29 May 2016.

91 M.K. Narayanan, 'The Jayalalithaa mystique', *The Hindu*, 21 December 2016.

92 First Post Staff, 'Jayalalithaa dead, A time line of events' First Post, December 6, 2016.

93 'UK doctor reveals details behind Jaya's death mystery', *The Economic Times*, 6 February 2017.

94 Online Desk, 'I don't think anyone has taken more criticism than I: Jaya told Simi Garewal', *The New Indian Express*, 6 December 2016.

95 Rollo Romig, 'What happens when a state is run by a movie star?' *New York Times*, 1 July 2015.

96 Telecast of an interview given in 2009, CNN News 18, 5 December 2016.

97 Wikileaks, 'Women in India: Tamil Nadu's iron lady J. Jayalalithaa', 9 March 2009.

98 Free Press Journal Bureau, 'Jaya explains why she is opposing GST', *Free Press Journal*, 1 June 2016.

99 T.S. Subramanian, 'Jayalalithaa's legacy', *Frontline*, 6 January 2017.

100 Prakash K.Dutta, 'Why funeral procession was on Tuesday after 4.30 PM', *India Today*, 5 December 2016.

101 Business Standard Reporter, 'Sasikala Natarajan brought Jayalalaihta down', *Business Standard*, 4 October 2014.

102 ibid.

103 Ibid.

104 Online Desk, 'I don't think anyone has taken more criticism than I: Jaya told Simi Garewal', *The New Indian Express*, 6 December 2016.

105 PTI, 'SC convicts Sasikala in DA case, dashes her bid to be Tamil Nadu CM', *Business Standard*, 14 February 2017.

106 Amarnath K. Menon, 'The Amma of all questions', *India Today*, 13 October 2016.

107 Ritu Sharma, 'Amma Alayam: Soon a temple for Tamil Nadu CM Jayalalihtaa', One India, 29 February 2016.

108 Phebha Mathew, 'AIADMK councillor builds temple in memory of goddess Jayalalithaa', *News Minute*, 15 December 2016.

109 K.V.Lakshmana, 'Trouble hit AIADMK eyes merger of warring factions, sidelines Sasikala and her kin, Hindustan Times, April 19.

110 Pioneer News Service, 'Dinakaran hints at quitting the party,' The Pioneer, April 20, 2.